MySQL Questions, Answers & Explanations:

MySQL Certification Prep

MySQL Questions, Answers & Explanations: MySQL
Certification Prep

978-1933804-59-9

Edited by Emilee Newman Bowles

Please visit our website at www.itcookbook.com

Table of Contents

Table of Contents.. 5
Question 1: MySQL 10
Question 2: Programming Languages Compatible with MySQL 11
Question 3: Uses of MySQL 12
Question 4: Administering MySQL.......................................12
Question 5: MySQL Platforms Compatibility..........................13
Question 6: Latest MySQL Version.......................................13
Question 7: MySQL Future Releases.....................................15
Question 8: Distinguishing Features of MySQL......................16
Question 9: Types of MySQL Server Compilations..................16
Question 10: MySQL Source Code Specifics............................17
Question 11: MySQL Technical Support.................................17
Question 12: MySQL Licensing 18
Question 14: Benefits of MySQL Certification....................... 23
Question 15: MySQL Certification Levels 24
Question 16: MySQL Versions in the Exam 25
Question 17: MySQL Version 4.0 or MySQL Version 4.1..........25
Question 18: Certification Exams Preparation.......................25
Question 19: Self-study for the Certification Exams............... 26
Question 20: Upgrading MySQL 4 Certifications....................27
Question 21: Length of Certification Validity.........................27
Question 22: MySQL Certification Study Guide..................... 28
Question 23: Venue of Certification Exams........................... 28
Question 24: Prerequisites for the MySQL 5.0 Certification
Exams.. 29
Question 25: Relationship between the Developer and DBA
Certifications.. 29
Question 26: Number of Exams Needed to Get Certification... 29
Question 27: Prerequisites for Taking the MySQL Core
Certification.. 30
Question 28: Prerequisites for Taking the MySQL Professional
Certification.. 30
Question 29: Closed Book Exams...31
Question 30: Duration of Certification Exams.......................31
Question 31: No Negative Score 31
Question 32: Retaking the Exams 32
Question 33: Certificate Copy 32
Question 34: Details of Exam Result 32
Question 35: Exam Cost.. 33
Question 36: MySQL Certification Developments.................. 33

Question 37: MySQL 5.0 and MySQL Cluster.......................... 33
Question 38: MySQL 5.0 Providing New Features/Capabilities
for MySQL Cluster.. 34
Question 39: MySQL 5.0 Include a Disk-based MySQL Cluster 34
Question 40: Using Cluster vs. Using Replication.....................35
Question 41: Special Networking to Run Cluster 36
Question 42: Number of Computers Needed to Run a Cluster. 36
Question 43: Functionality of Each Computer in a Cluster 37
Question 44: Hardware Requirements for Running MySQL
Cluster 38
Question 45: MySQL Cluster uses TCP/IP 38
Question 46: Querying Cluster.. 39
Question 47: Error or Warning Message when Using Cluster .. 40
Question 48: MySQL Cluster Transaction Safe........................ 40
Question 49: Storage Engines Supported by My SQL Cluster....41
Question 50: Versions of the MySQL Software that Support
Cluster 41
Question 51: Catastrophic Failure 42
Question 52: FULLTEXT Indexes with Cluster........................ 42
Question 53: Running Multiple Nodes on a Single Computer .. 43
Question 54: Add Nodes to a Cluster without Restarting It...... 44
Question 55: Limitations of Using Cluster.............................. 45
Question 56: Importing an Existing MySQL Database into a
Cluster 46
Question 57: Cluster Nodes Communication.......................... 46
Question 58: Arbitrator...47
Question 59: Data Types Supported by MySQL Cluster........... 48
Question 60: Different Kinds of Hardware and OS in a Cluster 49
Question 61: Hostnames with MySQL Cluster........................ 49
Question 62: Start and Stop MySQL Cluster 50
Question 63: MySQL 5.0 a Production/GA 50
Question 64: MySQL 5.0 Subqueries......................................51
Question 65: MySQL 5.0 Multi-table Inserts and Updates 51
Question 66: MySQL Query Cache..52
Question 67: MySQL 5.0 Sequences.......................................52
Question 68: MySQL 5.0 "NOW()" with Fractions of Seconds ..53
Question 69: MySQL 5.0 and Dual Core Opterons...................53
Question 70: MyISAM Hot-Backup.. 54
Question 71: Improvement in Error Reporting 54
Question 72: MySQL 5.0 and ACID Transactions 55
Question 73: Storage Engines in MySQL 5.0 55
Question 74: Unique Benefits of the ARCHIVE Storage Engine 56

Question 75: MySQL 5.0 New Features Apply to All the Storage Engines... 56
Question 76: Server SQL Mode 57
Question 77: Number of Modes in "Server SQL Mode" 57
Question 78: Configuring Server SQL Mode......................... 58
Question 79: Mode Dependency.. 58
Question 80: Extending "Strict Mode" Rules......................... 59
Question 81: "Strict Mode" Impact on Performance............... 59
Question 82: MySQL Default Mode...................................... 60
Question 83: Documentation and Forums for MySQL Stored Procedures 60
Question 84: ANSI SQL 2003 Specification for Stored Procedures 61
Question 85: Managing Stored Procedures............................ 61
Question 86: Viewing All Stored Procedures in a Database 62
Question 87: Stored Procedures Location............................. 62
Question 88: Grouping Stored Procedures............................ 63
Question 89: Stored Procedure Calling another Stored Procedure/Trigger.. 63
Question 90: Stored Procedure Accessing Tables 63
Question 91: Stored Procedures' "Raise" Statement............... 64
Question 92: Stored Procedures have Exception Handling...... 64
Question 93: Stored Procedures Return Result Sets............... 64
Question 94: "WITH RECOMPILE" for Stored Procedures 65
Question 95: MySQL Equivalent of Oracle's Use of mod_plsql 65
Question 96: Pass an Array as Input to a Stored Procedure 65
Question 97: Pass a Cursor as an IN Parameter to a Stored Procedure 66
Question 98: Cursor as an OUT parameter from a Stored Procedure 66
Question 99: Print out a Variable Value in a Stored Procedure for Debugging... 66
Question 100: Transaction inside a Stored Procedure............. 67
Question 101: Documentation and Forums for MySQL Triggers 67
Question 102: Statement-level Triggers and Row-level Triggers 68
Question 103: Default Triggers 68
Question 104: Managing Triggers 68
Question 105: View all Triggers in a Database 69
Question 106: Triggers Storage 70
Question 107: Trigger Calling a Stored Procedure................. 70
Question 108: Triggers Accessing a Single/Multiple Tables..... 70

Question 109: Triggers Calling an External Application........... 71
Question 110: Trigger Updating Tables on Remote Servers 71
Question 111: Documentation and Discussion Forum for MySQL
Views... 71
Question 112: Underlying Table is dropped........................... 72
Question 113: MySQL 5.0 Table Snapshots 72
Question 114: MySQL 5.0 Materialized Views 72
Question 115: Insert into Views Based on Joins 73
Question 116: Updating a View Affecting Multiple/Single table 73
Question 117: Documentation and Discussion Forum for MySQL
INFORMATION_SCHEMA 73
Question 119: Difference between the Oracle Data Dictionary and
MySQL INFORMATION_SCHEMA 74
Question 120: Groups of Tables in MySQL 75
Question 121: Tables in the INFORMATION_SCHEMA 75
Question 122: MySQL Connector/J and the New Features in
MySQL 5.0 75
Question 123: MySQL Connector/NET and the New Features in
MySQL 5.0 76
Question 124: MySQL Connector/ODBC and the New Features in
MySQL 5.0 76
Question 125: DBD: MySQL and the New Features in MySQL 5.0
.... 77
Question 126: MySQL and MySQLI extensions and the New
Features in MySQL 5.0.. 77
Question 127: Instance Manager Enable Management of Remote
MySQL Servers... 78
Question 128: Instance Manager on a Windows Machine........ 78
Question 129: GUI Tools Availability on Linux 79
Question 130: MySQL Administrator 80
and the New Features in MySQL 5.0 80
Question 131: MySQL Query Browser and the New Features in
MySQL 5.0 80
Question 132: MySQL GUI Tools to Build Stored Procedures and
Views... 80
Question 133: Backup/Restore and mysqldump Work with
Stored Procedures.. 81
Question 134: Mysqldump Actually Dump the Definitions of
Stored Procedures, Triggers, and Functions.......................... 81
Question 135: Migrate from MySQL 4.x to 5.0 82
Question 136: Table Types Change...................................... 83
Question 137: MySQL 5.0 Support for SSL........................... 84

Question 138: SSL Support for the MySQL Binaries 84
Question 139: MySQL 5.0 Built-in Authentication against LDAP Directories 85
Question 140: MySQL 5.0 Built-in Roles Based Access Control (RBAC) 85
Question 141: Benefits for an ISV/VAR to Embed MySQL into a Software or Hardware System... 86
Question 142: Scenarios for Embedding MySQL 87
Question 143: Key Relational Database Features that MySQL Provides.. 88
Question 144: Synchronization and Replication Capabilities of MySQL.. 89
Question 145: Performance and Scalability Characteristics of MySQL.. 91
Question 146: MySQL Reliability 92
Question 147: MySQL Easy to Administer............................. 93
Question 148: Minimum System Requirements for MySQL 93
Question 149: Platforms MySQL Support 94
Question 150: Industry Standards and 3rd Party Tools MySQL Support... 95
Question 151: MySQL Reduce TCO....................................... 97
Question 152: Pricing Model for Embedding MySQL 98
Question 153: ISV/VARs that currently embed MySQL 98
Question 154: Partner Program for Companies Interested in Embedding MySQL... 99
Question 155: Information about Embedding MySQL............. 99
Question 156: Primary Business Benefit that MySQL Provides 100
Question 157: Additional Benefits MySQL Provide 100
Question 158: MySQL Support ISV/VARs Who Want to Distribute MySQL.. 101
Scenario 2: Bundled MySQL 102
Question 159: Installed Base of MySQL 102
Question 160: Customer References for MySQL 103
Question 161: Fully Supported... 103
Question 162: Conditionally Supported 104
Question 163: Limited Support.. 104
Question 164: Who uses MySQL?... 105
Useful Links and Sites.. 114
Index 115

Question 1: MySQL

What is MySQL?

A: MySQL is a multi-threaded, multi-user, SQL Database Management System (DBMS) with more than six million installations. MySQL AB makes MySQL available as free software under the GNU General Public License (GPL), but they also dual-license it under traditional proprietary licensing arrangements for cases where the intended use is incompatible with the GPL.
MySQL is an open source product and works on many different platforms including AIX, BSDi, FreeBSD, HP-UX, Linux, Mac OS X, NetBSD, OpenBSD, OS/2 Warp, SGI IRIX, Solaris, SunOS, SCO OpenServer, SCO UnixWare, Tru64, Windows 95, Windows 98, Windows NT, Windows 2000, Windows XP, and more recent versions of Windows.

Unlike projects such as Apache, where the software is developed by a public community and the copyright to the codebase is owned by its individual authors, MySQL is owned and sponsored by a single for-profit firm, the Swedish company MySQL AB, which holds the copyright to most of the codebase. The company develops and maintains the system, sells support and service contracts, as well as proprietary-licensed copies of MySQL, and employs people all over the world who collaborate via the Internet. MySQL AB was founded by David Axmark, Allan Larsson, and Michael "Monty" Widenius.

Question 2: Programming Languages Compatible with MySQL

What programming languages are compatible with MySQL?

A: There are APIs available that allow applications written in numerous programming languages to access MySQL databases, including: C, C++, C#, Borland Delphi (via dbExpress), Eiffel, Smalltalk, Java (with a native Java driver implementation), Lisp, PERL, PHP, Python, Ruby, REALbasic (Mac), FreeBasic, and TCL. Each one of these uses a specific API. An ODBC interface called MyODBC allows additional programming languages that support the ODBC interface to communicate with a MySQL database, such as ASP. MySQL is mostly implemented in ANSI C, a common "lingua franca" for system libraries, and it tends to use that as its "native" language.

Question 3: Uses of MySQL

What are the uses of MySQL?

A: MySQL is popular for web applications such as MediaWiki or PHP-Nuke and acts as the database component of the LAMP and WAMP platforms (Linux/Windows-Apache-MySQL-PHP/Perl/Python). Its popularity as a web application is closely tied to the popularity of PHP, which is often combined with MySQL and nicknamed the Dynamic Duo. It is easy to find many references that link the two in websites and books (PHP and MySQL for Dummies, PHP and MySQL Bible, Beginning PHP and MySQL, etc.) The claim made in many books is that MySQL is easier to learn and use than many other database applications. For example, the Dummies book says you can quit MySQL with an obvious command of either exit or quit, but this is true for many other database applications.

Question 4: Administering MySQL

How do you administer MySQL?

A: To administer MySQL databases, one can use the included command-line tool (mysql and mysqladmin). GUI administration tools are also downlodable from the MySQL site: MySQL Administrator and MySQL Query Browser.

http://www.mysql.com/products/tools/administrator/

http://www.mysql.com/products/tools/query-browser/

A widespread and popular alternative, written in PHP, is the free software web application phpMyAdmin.

Question 5: MySQL Platforms Compatibility

What platforms do my MySQL work on?

A: MySQL works on many different platforms including AIX, BSDi, FreeBSD, HP-UX, GNU/Linux, Mac OS X, NetBSD, Novell NetWare, OpenBSD, OS/2 Warp, QNX, SGI IRIX, Solaris, SunOS, SCO OpenServer, SCO UnixWare, Tru64, Windows 95, Windows 98, Windows NT, Windows 2000, Windows XP, and more recent versions of Windows.

A port of MySQL to OpenVMS is also available

Question 6: Latest MySQL Version

What are the features of the latest MySQL?

A: As of May 2006, MySQL offers production version 5.0.22. It includes the following features:

> A broad subset of ANSI SQL 99, as well as extensions.

> Cross-platform support.

> Stored procedures.

> Triggers.

> Cursors.

> Updatable Views.

> True VARCHAR support.

> INFORMATION_SCHEMA.

> Strict mode.

> X/Open XA distributed transaction processing (DTP) support. Two phase commit as part of this, using Oracle's InnoDB Engine.

> Independent storage engines (MyISAM for read speed, InnoDB for transactions and referential integrity, and Archive for storing historical data in little space).

> Transactions with the "InnoDB," BDB, and Cluster storage engines; "savepoints" with "InnoDB."

> SSL support.

> Query caching.

> "Sub-SELECTs" (or nested "SELECTs").

> Replication with one master per slave, many slaves per master, no automatic support for multiple masters per slave.

> Full-text indexing and searching using MyISAM engine.

> Embedded database library.

> Full Unicode support.

> ACID compliance using the "InnoDB," BDB, and Cluster engines.

> Shared-nothing clustering through MySQL Cluster.

Question 7: MySQL Future Releases

Are there any plans for future versions/releases of MySQL?

A: Yes. The MySQL 5.1 roadmap outlines support for:

> Partitioning.

> Online backup for all storage engines.

> Fail-safe replication.

> Column-level constraints.

> Event Scheduling.

> XML functions.

Foreign key support for all storage engines will likely be released with MySQL 5.2 (although it has been present since version 3.23 for InnoDB). The current MySQL 5.1 development release is 5.1.11 beta.

Question 8: Distinguishing Features of MySQL

What are the distinguishing features of MySQL?

A: The following features are implemented by MySQL but not by other RDBMSes:

> Multiple storage engines (MyISAM, Merge, InnoDB, BDB, Memory/heap, Cluster, Federated, Archive, CSV, Blackhole and Example in 5.x), letting you choose the one which is most effective for each table in the application.

> Commit grouping, gathering multiple transactions from multiple connections together to increase the number of commits per second.

Question 9: Types of MySQL Server Compilations

How many server compilation types are there in MySQL?

A: There are 3 types of MySQL Server Compilations:

> Standard: The MySQL-Standard binaries are recommended for most users, and include the InnoDB storage engine.

> Max: (not MaxDB, which is a cooperation with SAP) is a mysqld-max Extended MySQL Server. The MySQL-Max binaries include additional features that may not have been as extensively tested or are not required for general usage.

> The MySQL-Debug binaries have been compiled with extra debug information and are not intended for production use because the included debugging code may cause reduced performance.

Question 10: MySQL Source Code Specifics

What are the source code specifics of MySQL?

A: MySQL is written in a mixture of C and C++. The SQL parser uses "yacc" and home-brewed "lexer."

Question 11: MySQL Technical Support

Does MySQL offer technical support?

A: Yes, via MySQL Network MySQL AB offers support itself, including 24/7 support with 30-minute response time, with the support team having direct access to the developers as necessary to handle problems. In addition, it hosts forums and mailing lists. Employees and other users are often available in several IRC channels providing assistance.

Members of the MySQL Network enjoy access to binaries and software that is certified for their particular operating system and the codebase changes much less frequently than the Community Edition of the MySQL Database Server engine. The Network maintains several levels of membership based on importance and urgency for response times.

Question 12: MySQL Licensing

What are the different types of MySQL licensing?

A: Both the MySQL server software itself and the client libraries are distributed under a dual-licensing format. Users may choose the GNU General Public License, which MySQL has extended with a FLOSS License Exception. It allows Software licensed under other OSI-compliant Open Source licences, which are not compatible to the GPL, to link against the MySQL client libraries.

Users that do not wish to be bound to the terms of the GPL may choose to purchase a proprietary license.

Some users have independently continued to develop an earlier version of the client libraries, which was distributed under the less-restrictive Lesser General Public License.

FLOSS License List

License name	Version/Copyright Date
Academic Free License	2.0
Apache Software License	1.0/1.1/2.0
Apache Public Source License	2.0
Artistic license	From Perl 5.8.0
BSD license	July 22, 1999
Common Public License	1.0
GNU Library or "Lesser" General Public License (LGPL)	2.0/2.1
Jabber Open Source License	1.0
MIT license	—
Mozilla Public License (MPL)	1.0/1.1
Open Software License	2.0
OpenSSL license with original SSLeay licenses	2003 ("1998")
PHP License	3.0
Python license (CNRI Python License)	2.1.1
Python Software Foundation License	1995
Sleepycat License	—
University of Illinois/NCSA Open Source License	—
W3C License	2001
X11 License	—
Zlib/libpng License	—
Zope Public License	2.0

MySQL 5.0 Reference Manual - K MySQL FLOSS License Exception - Microsoft Internet Explorer

File Edit View Favorites Tools Help

MySQL 5.0 Reference Manual

* MySQL Change History
* Porting to Other Systems
* Environment Variables
* Regular Expressions
* Limits in MySQL
* Feature Restrictions
* GNU General Public License
* MySQL FLOSS License Exception
* Index

Get the MySQL Reference Software and MySQL Administrator's Guide from MySQL Press!

Additional languages

* French
* Spanish

Get Support with MySQL Network today!

Order from our online shop and get technical support from MySQL engineers today.

Get Support Now »

Learn about new MySQL releases, browse archives, events and more.

FLOSS License List

License name	Version(s)/Copyright Date
Academic Free License	2.0
Apache Software License	1.0/1.2.0
Apple Public Source License	2.0
Artistic license	From Perl 5.8.0
BSD license	July 22 1999*
Common Public License	1.0
GNU Library or "Lesser" General Public License (LGPL)	2.0/2.1
Jabber Open Source License	1.0
MIT license	
Mozilla Public License (MPL)	1.0/1.1
Open Software License	2.0
OpenSSL license (with original SSLeay license)	2003* ("1998")
PHP License	3.0
Python license (CNRI Python License)	
Python Software Foundation License	2.1.1
Sleepycat License	1999
University of Illinois/NCSA Open Source License	
W3C License	2001*
X11 License	2001*
Zlib/libpng License	
Zope Public License	2.0

Due to the many versions of some of the above licenses, we require that any version follow the 2003 version of the Free Software Foundation, Free Software Definition ...

21

FLOSS License List

License name	Version(s)/Copyright Date
Academic Free License	2.0
Apache Software License	1.0/1.1/2.0
Apple Public Source License	2.0
Artistic license	From Perl 5.8.0
BSD license	July 22, 1999*
Common Public License	1.0
GNU Library or "Lesser" General Public License (LGPL)	2.0/2.1
Jabber Open Source License	1.0
MIT license	—
Mozilla Public License (MPL)	1.0/1.1
Open Software License	2.0
OpenSSL license (with original SSLeay license)	2003* (*1998*)
PHP License	3.0
Python license (CNRI Python License)	—
Python Software Foundation License	2.1.1
Sleepycat License	1999
University of Illinois/NCSA Open Source License	—
W3C License	2001*
X11 License	2001*
Zlib/libpng License	—
Zope Public License	2.0

Due to the many variants of some of the above licenses, we require that any version follow the 2003 version of the Free Software ...

- 7. MySQL Change Notes
- F. Errors in Other Clients
- F. Environment Variables
- G. Regular Expressions
- H. Limits in MySQL
- I. Feature Restrictions
- J. GNU General Public License
- K. MySQL FLOSS License Exception
- Index

Get the MySQL Language Reference and MySQL Administrator's Guide from MySQL Press!

Additional languages

- French
- Spanish

Get Support with MySQL Network (today)

Order from our online store and get technical support from MySQL engineers today.

Get Support Now »

Learn about new MySQL releases, technical articles, events and more.

Question 13: MySQL Certification

What is MySQL Certification?

A: The MySQL Certification Program is a high quality certification program that provides developers and DBAs with the credentials to prove they have the knowledge, experience, and skills to use and manage MySQL Server.

Question 14: Benefits of MySQL Certification

What are the benefits of MySQL Certification?

A: MySQL Developer and DBA Certifications provide developers and DBAs with the following benefits:

> Better recognition of your skills. As a MySQL certified user you can expect many benefits because your skills have been confirmed by a neutral testing body.

> Get a better position. Certification gives you the edge when being considered for a promotion or other career opportunities. Receiving your certification shows you have the knowledge and skills to accept more responsibility.

> Establishes professional credentials. Certification stands out on your resume. It servs as an impartial, third-party endorsement to your knowledge and experience.

Question 15: MySQL Certification Levels

What are the certification levels?

A: There are two levels of certification in the MySQL AB Certification Program for MySQL 5.0:

> MySQL Developer Certification is proof that you know and are able to make use of all the features of MySQL that are needed to develop and maintain applications that use MySQL for back-end storage.

> The MySQL Database Administrator Certification attests that you know how to maintain and optimize an installation of one or more MySQL servers and perform administrative tasks such as monitoring the server, making backups, and so forth.

There are also two levels of certification in the MySQL AB Certification Program for MySQL 4:

> MySQL Core Certification proves you have mastered the fundamental skills of using MySQL including creating and using databases and tables, inserting, modifying, deleting, and retrieving data.

> MySQL Professional Certification proves you have mastered the ability to manage MySQL Server including such advanced areas of database management, installation, security, disaster prevention, and optimization.

Question 16: MySQL Versions in the Exam

Exactly what versions of MySQL are targeted in the 5.0 exams?

A: The exam questions all presume that you are using a stock installation of a production version (i.e., 5.0.15 or higher), as downloaded from the MySQL web sites.

Question 17: MySQL Version 4.0 or MySQL Version 4.1

Do the exams target MySQL version 4.0 or MySQL version 4.1?

A: Since early 2005, these exams have been based on MySQL version 4.1.

Question 18: Certification Exams Preparation

How do I best prepare for the certification exams?

A: For MySQL version 5.0, MySQL AB provides several training courses that prepare you for the MySQL 5.0 certificiation exams. The courses MySQL 5.0 for Developers and MySQL 5.0 for DBAs are both closely aligned with the contents of these exams. Please visit the links below for more details:

http://www.mysql.com/training/workshops/mysql_dev.html

http://www.mysql.com/training/workshops/mysql_dba.h
tml

As for MySQL version 4.0, MySQL AB provides several
training courses that prepare you for the MySQL 4
certificiation exams. The course *Using and Managing
MySQL* is closely aligned with the contents of these exams.

Question 19: Self-study for the Certification Exams

Where can I best do self-study for the certification exams?

A: MySQL Press has published the MySQL Certification
Study Guide for exactly this purpose. It is available from
several on-line bookstores as well as in most bookstores in
the world that specialize in literature for technical fields.
You can visit the link below for more details:

http://www.mysql.com/training/certificationstudyguides/
index.html

Question 20: Upgrading MySQL 4 Certifications

Is it recommended to upgrade my certification from MySQL 4 to MySQL5?

A: If you already hold a MySQL 4 certification, you should consider upgrading it to MySQL 5.0. MySQL AB will provide upgraded exams, in which you take a single exam to upgrade your MySQL 4 certification to the MySQL 5.0 certifications. If you are MySQL 4 Core certified, you may upgrade to MySQL 5.0 Developer. If you are MySQL Professional Certified, you may upgrade to MySQL 5 DBA.

Upgrade exams are available when the regular certification exams move from Beta to General Availability.

Question 21: Length of Certification Validity

How long are the Certifications valid?

A: MySQL certifications are tied to the version numbers of the MySQL server and related products. A change in the version number is made by MySQL AB when significant new features are introduced in MySQL server.

As older versions become outdated, MySQL AB will retire the certifications related to these versions. Candidates will be notified well in advance when such a retirement will take place.

At MySQL AB, we believe that although certifications help you prove your knowledge, certification is no substitute for experience. Nonetheless, prospective employers are likely to look more favorably at candidates who continually keep updated on their knowledge and recertifying will help you with that proof.

Question 22: MySQL Certification Study Guide

I bought the MySQL Certification Study Guide, but that does not seem to cover features in MySQL4.1. Why is this?

A: In order to save you money, we chose to make a small addendum instead, which you can download at:

http://www.mysql.com/training/certification/studyguides/

Question 23: Venue of Certification Exams

Where will I be able to take certification exams?

A: Person VUE, who delivers MySQL AB exams, has more than 3.000 test centers world-wide. Use their test center locator at the link below to find one:

http://www.vue.com/servlet/vue.web2.core.Dispatcher?w ebContext=CandidateSite&webApp=TestCenterLocator&re questedAction=register&cid=271

Question 24: Prerequisites for the MySQL 5.0 Certification Exams

What are the prerequisites for the MySQL 5.0 certification exams?

A: There are no formal prerequisites for taking MySQL 5.0 certification exams, although having some working experience is obviously needed.

Question 25: Relationship between the Developer and DBA Certifications

The MySQL 4 exams have core certification as a prerequisite for taking the professional exam. Is there a similar relationship between the Developer and DBA certifications?

A: No. In the MySQL 5.0 exam structure, the Developer and DBA exams are considered separate.

Question 26: Number of Exams Needed to Get Certification

How many exams do I need to pass to attain a certification?

A: Each level of certification for the MySQL 5.0 certifications requires you to take two exams. The two exams for a particular certification may be taken in any order.

Each level of certification for the MySQL 4 certifications requires you to take one exam.

Question 27: Prerequisites for Taking the MySQL Core Certification

What are the prerequisites for taking the exam for the MySQL Core Certification?

A: None, although having some experience with MySQL is obviously needed. We recommend that you have at least 150 hours worth of experience working with MySQL.

Question 28: Prerequisites for Taking the MySQL Professional Certification

What are the prerequisites for taking the exam for the MySQL Professional Certification?

A: You must have attained the MySQL Core Certification before signing up for the MySQL Professional Certification exam. You should also have a lot more experience working with MySQL.

Question 29: Closed Book Exams

Can I bring the manual or other books to the exam?

A: The exams are designed to be closed book so you will not need (or be allowed) to bring any materials with you to the exam.

Question 30: Duration of Certification Exams

How long are the Certification Exams?

A: The test session length is 90 minutes. During this time, you're presented with 70 questions. You should attempt to answer all questions because an unanswered question will count as a wrong answer. You can move back and forth between questions, so initially you can skip the ones you're unsure of and return to them as time permits.

Question 31: No Negative Score

If I don't know the answer to a question, is it better to guess or should I leave it unanswered?

A: You do not get a "negative score" for wrongly answered questions. Thus, you should always attempt to answer a question.

Question 32: Retaking the Exams

If I failed the exams can I take them again?

A: Exams may be retaken at any time. However, if you fail an exam, MySQL AB strongly recommends that you spend at least two weeks doing extra studies for an exam before you retake it. All exams are created on-the-fly from a large pool of questions, and thus it is unlikely that you'll be presented with any of the questions you answered in the first try.

Question 33: Certificate Copy

When will I receive my certificate?

A: Your certificate will arrive by postal mail 4 to 6 weeks after you passed the exam. For Beta exams, the review process is quite a bit longer, so for these you will need to have a bit more patience.

Question 34: Details of Exam Result

I went to an exam, and all I was told was whether I had passed or failed the exam. How do I find out the details of how I did?

A: Currently, MySQL AB does not release detailed information on the scores of the MySQL 4 exams.

Question 35: Exam Cost

How much do the exams cost?

A: All MySQL certification exams are offered at the local equivalent of US$200 / EUR170.

Question 36: MySQL Certification Developments

How do I stay updated on the latest MySQL certification developments?

A: Subscribe to the MySQL Certification mailing list to stay updated on the latest MySQL Certification developments. Send an e-mail to the address below to subscribe.

certification-subscribe@lists.mysql.com

Question 37: MySQL 5.0 and MySQL Cluster

Does MySQL 5.0 work with MySQL Cluster?

A: Yes, MySQL 5.0 works with MySQL Cluster.

Question 38: MySQL 5.0 Providing New Features/Capabilities for MySQL Cluster

Does MySQL 5.0 provide any new features or capabilities for MySQL Cluster?

A: MySQL Cluster in 5.0 introduces various speed optimizations as well as decreased memory usage. See the link below for more details.

http://dev.mysql.com/doc/mysql/en/mysql-5-0-cluster-changes.html

Question 39: MySQL 5.0 Include a Disk-based MySQL Cluster

Does MySQL 5.0 include a disk-based MySQL Cluster?

A: Not yet. Essential infrastructure for this feature is currently under development, but the full feature is scheduled on the MySQL roadmap as a "rolling feature." This means that it is not a flagship feature, but will be implemented, development time permitting. Specific customer demand may change this scheduling. Visit the website below for more details.

http://dev.mysql.com/doc/mysql/en/mysql-5-1-cluster-roadmap.html

Question 40: Using Cluster vs. Using Replication

What's the difference between using cluster versus using replication?

A: In a replication setup, a master MySQL server updates one or more slaves. Transactions are committed sequentially and a slow transaction can cause the slave to lag behind the master. This means that if the master fails, it is possible that the slave might not have recorded the last few transactions. If a transaction-safe engine such as InnoDB is being used, a transaction will either be complete on the slave or not applied at all, but replication does not guarantee that all data on the master and the slave will be consistent at all times. In MySQL Cluster, all data nodes are kept in synchrony, and a transaction committed by any one data node is committed for all data nodes. In the event of a data node failure, all remaining data nodes remain in a consistent state.

In short, whereas standard MySQL replication is asynchronous, MySQL Cluster is synchronous.

We have implemented (asynchronous) replication for Cluster in MySQL 5.1. This includes the capability to replicate both between two clusters, and from a MySQL cluster to a non-Cluster MySQL server. However, we do not plan to "backport" this functionality to MySQL 5.0.

Question 41: Special Networking to Run Cluster

Do I need to do any special networking to run Cluster?

How do computers in a cluster communicate?

A: MySQL Cluster is intended to be used in a high-bandwidth environment, with computers connecting via TCP/IP. Its performance depends directly upon the connection speed between the cluster's computers. The minimum connectivity requirements for Cluster include a typical 100-megabit Ethernet network or the equivalent. We recommend you use gigabit Ethernet whenever it is available.

The faster SCI protocol is also supported, but requires special hardware.

Question 42: Number of Computers Needed to Run a Cluster

How many computers do I need to run a cluster and why?

A: A minimum of three computers is required to run a viable cluster. However, the minimum recommended number of computers in a MySQL Cluster is four: one each to run the management and SQL nodes and two computers to serve as data nodes. The purpose of the two data nodes is to provide redundancy. The management node must run on a separate machine to guarantee continued arbitration services in the event that one of the data nodes fails.

Question 43: Functionality of Each Computer in a Cluster

What do the different computers do in a cluster?

A: A MySQL Cluster has both a physical and a logical organization, with computers being the physical elements. The logical or functional elements of a cluster are referred to as nodes, and a computer housing a cluster node is sometimes referred to as a cluster host. Ideally, there will be one node per cluster host, although it is possible to run multiple nodes on a single host. There are three types of nodes, each corresponding to a specific role within the cluster. They are:

> Management node (MGM node): Provides management services for the cluster as a whole, including startup, shutdown, backups, and configuration data for the other nodes. The management node server is implemented as the application ndb_mgmd. The management client used to control MySQL Cluster via the MGM node is ndb_mgm.

> Data node: Stores and replicates data. Data node functionality is handled by an instance of the NDB data node process ndbd.

> SQL node: This is simply an instance of MySQL Server (mysqld) that is built with support for the NDB Cluster storage engine and started with the --ndb-cluster option to enable the engine.

Question 44: Hardware Requirements for Running MySQL Cluster

What are the hardware requirements for running a MySQL Cluster?

A: Cluster should run on any platform for which NDB-enabled binaries are available. Naturally, faster CPUs and more memory will improve performance and 64-bit CPUs will likely be more effective than 32-bit processors. There must be sufficient memory on machines used for data nodes to hold each node's share of the database. Nodes can communicate via a standard TCP/IP network and hardware. For SCI support, special networking hardware is required.

Question 45: MySQL Cluster uses TCP/IP

Since MySQL Cluster uses TCP/IP, does that mean I can run it over the Internet with one or more nodes in a remote location?

A: It is very doubtful in any case that a cluster would perform reliably under such conditions, as MySQL Cluster was designed and implemented with the assumption that it would be run under conditions guaranteeing dedicated high-speed connectivity such as that found in a LAN setting using 100 Mbps or gigabit Ethernet (preferably the latter). We neither test nor warrant its performance using anything slower than this.

Also, it is extremely important to keep in mind that communications between the nodes in a MySQL Cluster are not secure, they are neither encrypted nor safeguarded by any other protective mechanism. The most secure configuration for a cluster is in a private network behind a firewall, with no direct access to any Cluster data or management nodes from the outside. For SQL nodes, you should take the same precautions as you would with any other instance of the MySQL server.

Question 46: Querying Cluster

Do I have to learn a new programming or query language to use Cluster?

A: No. Although some specialized commands are used to manage and configure the cluster itself, only standard MySQL queries and commands are required for the following operations:

> Creating, altering, and dropping tables.

> Inserting, updating, and deleting table data.

> Creating, changing, and dropping primary and unique indexes.

> Configuring and managing SQL nodes (MySQL servers).

Question 47: Error or Warning Message when Using Cluster

How do I find out what an error or warning message means when using Cluster?

A: There are two ways that this can be done:

> From within the MySQL client use SHOW ERRORS or SHOW WARNINGSimmediately upon being notified of the error or warning condition. Errors and warnings also are displayed in MySQL Query Browser.

> From a system shell prompt, use "perror --ndb error_code."

Question 48: MySQL Cluster Transaction Safe

Is MySQL Cluster transaction safe? What isolation levels are supported?

A: Yes. For tables created with the NDB storage engine, transactions are supported. In MySQL 5.0, Cluster supports only the READ COMMITTED transaction isolation level.

Question 49: Storage Engines Supported by MySQL Cluster

What storage engines are supported by MySQL Cluster?

A: Clustering in MySQL is supported only by the NDB storage engine. That is, in order for a table to be shared between nodes in a cluster, it must be created using ENGINE=NDB (or ENGINE=NDBCLUSTER, which is equivalent). (It is possible to create tables using other storage engines such as "MyISAM" or "InnoDB" on a MySQL server being used for clustering, but these non-NDB tables will not participate in the cluster.)

Question 50: Versions of the MySQL Software that Support Cluster

Which versions of the MySQL software support Cluster?

Do I have to compile from source?

A: Cluster is supported in all MySQL-max binaries in the 5.0 release series, except as noted in the following paragraph. You can determine whether your server has NDB support using either the SHOW VARIABLES LIKE "have_%" or SHOW ENGINES statement. See following link for more information.

http://dev.mysql.com/doc/refman/5.0/en/mysqld-max.html

For Linux users, please note that NDB is not included in the standard MySQL server "RPMs." Beginning with MySQL 5.0.4, there are separate RPM packages for the NDB storage engine and accompanying management and other tools. See the NDB RPM Downloads section of the

MySQL 5.0 Downloads page for these. (Prior to 5.0.4, you had to use the -max binaries supplied as ".tar.gz" archives. This is still possible, but is not required, so you can use your Linux distribution's RPM manager if you prefer.) You can also obtain NDB support by compiling the -max binaries from source, but it is not necessary to do so simply to use MySQL Cluster. To download the latest binary, RPM, or source distribution in the MySQL 5.0 series, visit the link below.

http://dev.mysql.com/downloads/mysql/5.0.html

Question 51: Catastrophic Failure

In the event of a catastrophic failure, say, for instance, the whole city loses power and my UPS fails, would I lose all my data?

A: All committed transactions are logged. Therefore, although it is possible that some data could be lost in the event of a catastrophe, the loss should be limited. Data loss can be further reduced by minimizing the number of operations per transaction. It is not a good idea to perform large numbers of operations per transaction in any case.

Question 52: FULLTEXT Indexes with Cluster

Is it possible to use FULLTEXT indexes with Cluster?

A: FULLTEXT indexing is not currently supported by the NDB storage engine or by any storage engine other than

"MyISAM." We are working to add this capability in a future release.

Question 53: Running Multiple Nodes on a Single Computer

Can I run multiple nodes on a single computer?

A: It is possible but not advisable. One of the chief reasons to run a cluster is to provide redundancy. To enjoy the full benefits of this redundancy, each node should reside on a separate machine. If you place multiple nodes on a single machine and that machine fails, you lose all of those nodes. Given that MySQL Cluster can be run on commodity hardware loaded with a low-cost (or even no-cost) operating system, the expense of an extra machine or two is well worth it to safeguard mission critical data. It is also worth noting that the requirements for a Cluster host running a management node are minimal. This task can be accomplished with a 200 MHz Pentium CPU and sufficient RAM for the operating system plus a small amount of overhead for the "ndb_mgmd" and "ndb_mgm" processes.

Question 54: Add Nodes to a Cluster without Restarting It

Can I add nodes to a cluster without restarting it?

A: Not at the present time. A simple restart is all that is required for adding new MGM or SQL nodes to a Cluster. When adding data nodes the process is more complex and requires the following steps:

> Make a complete backup of all Cluster data.

> Completely shut down the cluster and all cluster node processes.

> Restart the cluster, using the "--initial startup" option.

> Restore all cluster data from the backup.

In a future MySQL Cluster release series, we hope to implement a "hot" reconfiguration capability for MySQL Cluster to minimize (if not eliminate) the requirement for restarting the cluster when adding new nodes.

Question 55: Limitations of Using Cluster

Are there any limitations when using Cluster?

A: NDB tables in MySQL are subject to these limitations:

> Not all character sets and collations are supported.

> FULLTEXT indexes and index prefixes are not supported. Only complete columns may be indexed.

> Spatial data types are not supported.

> Only complete rollbacks for transactions are supported. Partial rollbacks and rollbacks to "savepoints" are not supported.

> The max number of attributes allowed per table is 128 and attribute names cannot be longer than 31 characters. For each table, the max combined length of the table and database names is 122 characters.

> The maximum size for a table row is 8 kilobytes, not counting BLOB values. There is no set limit for the number of rows per table. Table size limits depend on a number of factors, in particular on the amount of RAM available to each data node.

> The NDB engine does not support foreign key constraints. With "MyISAM" tables, they are ignored.

> Query caching is not supported.

For additional information on Cluster limitations, see:

http://dev.mysql.com/doc/refman/5.0/en/mysql-cluster-limitations.html

Question 56: Importing an Existing MySQL Database into a Cluster

How do I import an existing MySQL database into a cluster?

A: You can import databases into MySQL Cluster much as you would with any other version of MySQL. Other than the limitation mentioned in the previous question, the only other special requirement is that any tables included in the cluster must use the NDB storage engine. This means the tables must be created with "ENGINE=NDB" or "ENGINE=NDBCLUSTER." It is also possible to convert existing tables using other storage engines to NDB Cluster using ALTER TABLE, but requires an additional workaround.

Question 57: Cluster Nodes Communication

How do cluster nodes communicate with one another?

A: Cluster nodes can communicate via any of three different protocols: TCP/IP, SHM (shared memory), or SCI (Scalable Coherent Interface). Where available, SHM is used by default between nodes residing on the same cluster host. SCI is a high-speed (1 gigabit per second and higher), high-availability protocol used in building scalable multi-processor systems. It requires special hardware and drivers. For more about using SCI as a transport mechanism in MySQL Cluster, see the webpage below.

http://dev.mysql.com/doc/refman/5.0/en/mysql-cluster-interconnects.html

Question 58: Arbitrator

What is an Arbitrator?

A: If one or more nodes in a cluster fail, it is possible that not all cluster nodes will be able to "see" one another. In fact, it is possible that two sets of nodes might become isolated from one another in a network partitioning, also known as a "split brain" scenario. This type of situation is undesirable because each set of nodes tries to behave as though it is the entire cluster.

When cluster nodes go down, there are two possibilities. If more than 50% of the remaining nodes can communicate with each other, we have what is sometimes called a "majority rules" situation, and this set of nodes is considered to be the cluster. The arbitrator comes into play when there is an even number of nodes: in such cases, the set of nodes that the arbitrator belongs to is considered to be the cluster and nodes not belonging to this set are shut down.

The preceding information is somewhat simplified. A more complete explanation taking into account node groups follows:

When all nodes in at least one node group are alive, network partitioning is not an issue, because no one portion of the cluster can form a functional cluster. The real problem arises when no single node group has all its nodes alive, in which case network partitioning (the "split-brain" scenario) becomes possible. Then an arbitrator is required. All cluster nodes recognize the same node as the arbitrator, which is normally the management server. However, it is possible to configure any of the MySQL Servers in the cluster to act as the arbitrator instead. The arbitrator accepts the first set of cluster nodes to contact it, and tells the remaining set to shut down. Arbitrator selection is controlled by the ArbitrationRank configuration parameter for MySQL Server and management server nodes. It should also be noted that the role of arbitrator does not in and of itself impose any heavy demands upon the host so designated, and thus the arbitrator host does not need to be particularly fast or to have extra memory especially for this purpose. See the webpage below for more details.

http://dev.mysql.com/doc/refman/5.0/en/mysql-cluster-mgm-definition.html

Question 59: Data Types Supported by MySQL Cluster

What data types are supported by MySQL Cluster?

A: MySQL Cluster supports all of the usual MySQL data types, with the exception of those associated with MySQL spatial extensions. See the following link for details:

http://dev.mysql.com/doc/refman/5.0/en/spatial-extensions.html

In addition, there are some differences with regard to indexes when used with NDB tables.

Note: MySQL Cluster tables (that is, tables created with ENGINE=NDBCLUSTER) have only fixed-width rows. This means that (for example) each record containing a VARCHAR (255) column will require space for 255 characters (as required for the character set and collation being used for the table), regardless of the actual number of characters stored therein. This issue is expected to be fixed in a future MySQL release series. See the link below for more details.

http://dev.mysql.com/doc/refman/5.0/en/mysql-cluster-limitations.html

Question 60: Different Kinds of Hardware and OS in a Cluster

Can I mix different kinds of hardware and operating systems in a Cluster?

A: Yes, so long as all machines and operating systems have the same "endianness" (all big-endian or all little-endian). It is also possible to use different MySQL Cluster releases on different nodes. However, we recommend this be done only as part of a rolling upgrade procedure.

Question 61: Hostnames with MySQL Cluster

Can I use hostnames with MySQL Cluster?

A: Yes, it is possible to use DNS and DHCP for cluster hosts. However, if your application requires "five nines" availability, we recommend using fixed IP addresses. Making communication between Cluster hosts dependent on services such as DNS and DHCP introduces additional points of failure, and the fewer of these the better.

Question 62: Start and Stop MySQL Cluster

How do I start and stop MySQL Cluster?

A: It is necessary to start each node in the cluster separately, in the following order:

> Start the management node with the "ndb_mgmd" command.

> Start each data node with the "ndbd" command.

> Start each MySQL server (SQL node) using "mysqld_safe --user=mysql &."

Each of these commands must be run from a system shell on the machine housing the affected node. You can verify the cluster is running by starting the MGM management client "ndb_mgm" on the machine housing the MGM node.

Question 63: MySQL 5.0 a Production/GA

When did MySQL 5.0 become Production/GA?

A: MySQL 5.0 released a Production on October 19, 2005. We are now working on MySQL 5.1, which is in the alpha stages.

Question 64: MySQL 5.0 Subqueries

Can MySQL 5.0 do subqueries?

A: Yes. MySQL supports subqueries since version 4.1. See the link below for more information.

http://dev.mysql.com/doc/mysql/en/subqueries.html

Question 65: MySQL 5.0 Multi-table Inserts and Updates

Can MySQL 5.0 do multi-table inserts and updates?

A: Yes. Multi-table UPDATE and DELETE were actually implemented in MySQL 4.0, with enhancements added in MySQL 4.1. See the links below for details.

http://dev.mysql.com/doc/mysql/en/UPDATE.html

http://dev.mysql.com/doc/mysql/en/DELETE.html

Question 66: MySQL Query Cache

Does MySQL 5.0 have a Query Cache? Does it work on
Server, Instance, or Database?

A: Yes. The Query Cache was introduced in MySQL 4.0,
and operates on the server level. It caches complete result
sets, matched with the original query string. If an exactly
identical query is made (which often happens, particularly
in web applications), no parsing or execution is necessary
because the result is sent directly from the cache. Various
tuning options are available. Please visit the link below.

http://dev.mysql.com/doc/mysql/en/query-cache.html

Question 67: MySQL 5.0 Sequences

Does MySQL 5.0 have Sequences?

A: No. However, MySQL has an "AUTO_INCREMENT"
system, which in MySQL 5.0 can also handle inserts in a
multi-master replication setup. With the "--auto-
increment-increment" and "-auto-increment-offset"
startup options, you can set each server to generate auto-
increment values that don't conflict with other servers.
The "auto-increment-increment" should be >= the number
of servers and each server should have a unique offset.

Question 68: MySQL 5.0 "NOW()" with Fractions of Seconds

Does MySQL 5.0 have a "NOW()" with fractions of seconds?

A: No. This is on the MySQL roadmap as a "rolling feature." This means that it is not a flagship feature, but will be implemented, development time permitting. Specific customer demand may change this scheduling.

MySQL will, however, parse time strings with a fractional component. See the link below for more details.

http://dev.mysql.com/doc/mysql/en/time.html

Question 69: MySQL 5.0 and Dual Core Opterons

Does MySQL 5.0 work with Dual Core Opterons?

A: Yes. MySQL is fully multi-threaded and will make use of multiple CPUs provided the operating system supports it.

Question 70: MyISAM Hot-Backup

Is there a "MyISAM Hot-Backup" like the "InnoDB Hot-Backup"?

A: This is currently under development and scheduled for MySQL 5.1.

Question 71: Improvement in Error Reporting

Is there any improvement in error reporting when Foreign Key fails (i.e., currently does not report which column and reference failed)?

A: The foreign key support in InnoDB has seen improvements in each major version of MySQL. However, global foreign key support (i.e., generically for all storage engines) is scheduled for MySQL 5.2 and should resolve any inadequacies in the current storage engine specific implementation.

Question 72: MySQL 5.0 and ACID Transactions

Can MySQL 5.0 do ACID Transactions?

A: Yes. MySQL has supported transactions for years now, since 3.23-Max and all versions 4.0 and above. The InnoDB storage engine offers full ACID transactions with row-level locking, multi-versioning, non-locking repeatable reads, and all four SQL standard isolation levels.

Question 73: Storage Engines in MySQL 5.0

What are the new Storage Engines in MySQL 5.0?

A: The FEDERATED storage engine, new in MySQL 5.0, allows the server to access tables in other (remote) servers. See the link below for details.

http://dev.mysql.com/doc/mysql/en/federated-storage-engine.html

MySQL 4.1 already added other new storage engines, such as ARCHIVE, CSV, and NDB (Cluster).

Question 74: Unique Benefits of the ARCHIVE Storage Engine

What are the unique benefits of the ARCHIVE Storage Engine?

A: The ARCHIVE Storage Engine, added in MySQL 4.1, is ideally suited for storing large amounts of data (without indexes) in a very small footprint and selects using table scans. See the link below for details.

http://dev.mysql.com/doc/mysql/en/archive-storage-engine.html

Question 75: MySQL 5.0 New Features Apply to All the Storage Engines

Do the new features in MySQL 5.0 apply to all the Storage Engines?

A: The general new features such as views, stored procedures, triggers, INFORMATION_SCHEMA, precision math (DECIMAL column type), and the BIT column type, apply to all storage engines. There are also additions and changes for specific storage engines.

Question 76: Server SQL Mode

What is Server SQL Mode?

A: The MySQL server can operate in different SQL modes and (as of MySQL 4.1) can apply these modes separately for different clients. Modes define what SQL syntax MySQL should support and what kind of data validation checks it should perform. This makes it easier to use MySQL in different environments and to use MySQL together with other database servers. For more information, see:

http://dev.mysql.com/doc/mysql/en/server-sql-mode.html

Question 77: Number of Modes in "Server SQL Mode"

How many modes are there in "Server SQL Mode"?

A: Quite a few, as each mode can be individually switched on and off. See the link below for a full current list.

http://dev.mysql.com/doc/mysql/en/server-sql-mode.html

Question 78: Configuring Server SQL Mode

How do you configure Server SQL Mode?

A: You can set the default SQL mode (for mysqld startup) in the MySQL configuration with the "--sql-mode" option. With SET [SESSION|GLOBAL] sql_mode='modes' you can change the settings from within a connection, either local to the connection or to take effect globally. You can retrieve the current mode by issuing a "SELECT @@sql_mode" statement.

Question 79: Mode Dependency

Is the mode dependent on the Database or the Connection?

A: A mode is not "linked" to a particular database. Modes can be set locally to the session (connection), or globally for the server With SET [SESSION|GLOBAL] sql_mode='modes' you can change the settings.

Question 80: Extending "Strict Mode" Rules

Can "Strict Mode" rules be extended?

A: Yes. When we refer to "strict mode," we mean a mode where at least one of "TRADITIONAL," "STRICT_TRANS_TABLES," or "STRICT_ALL_TABLES" is enabled. See the link below for more details.

http://dev.mysql.com/doc/mysql/en/server-sql-mode.html

Options can be combined, so you can add additional restrictions to a mode.

Question 81: "Strict Mode" Impact on Performance

Does "Strict Mode" impact performance?

A: Yes. A setting such as the requirement for detailed validation of input data requires some additional time. While the performance impact is not that great, if you do not require such validation (perhaps your application already handles all of this), MySQL gives you the option of leaving "Strict Mode" disabled. But if you do require it, "Strict Mode" delivers the validation you need.

Question 82: MySQL Default Mode

What is the default mode when MySQL 5.0 is installed?

A: By default, no special modes are enabled. For information about all available modes and the default behaviour in MySQL 5.0, visit the link below.

http://dev.mysql.com/doc/mysql/en/server-sql-mode.html

Question 83: Documentation and Forums for MySQL Stored Procedures

Where can I find documentation and forums for MySQL Stored Procedures?

A: You can find documentation for "MySQL Stored Procedures" in the "MySQL Reference Manual." This manual is accessible at:

http://dev.mysql.com/doc/mysql/en/stored-procedures.html

The discussion forums can be found at:

http://forums.mysql.com/list.php?98

Question 84: ANSI SQL 2003 Specification for Stored Procedures

Where can I find the ANSI SQL 2003 specification for Stored Procedures?

A: The official specifications are not freely available. ANSI makes them available for purchase. There are books available, such as *SQL-99 Complete, Really* by Peter Gulutzan and Trudy Pelzer, which give a comprehensive overview of the standard including stored procedures.

Question 85: Managing Stored Procedures

How do you manage Stored Procedures?

A: It is always good practice to use a clear naming scheme for your stored procedures. You can manage stored procedures with:

CREATE [FUNCTION|PROCEDURE], ALTER [FUNCTION|PROCEDURE]

DROP [FUNCTION|PROCEDURE]

SHOW CREATE [FUNCTION|PROCEDURE]

INFORMATION_SCHEMA

See the link below for more details.

http://dev.mysql.com/doc/mysql/en/routines-table.html

Question 86: Viewing All Stored Procedures in a Database

Is there a way to view all Stored Procedures in a database?

A: Yes, using the INFORMATION_SCHEMA.ROUTINES table: SELECT ROUTINE_TYPE, ROUTINE_NAME FROM INFORMATION_SCHEMA.ROUTINES WHERE ROUTINE_SCHEMA='dbname'. See the following link.

http://dev.mysql.com/doc/mysql/en/routines-table.html

The body of individual stored procedures can be seen through "SHOW CREATE [FUNCTION|PROCEDURE]" "procname." See the following link for details.

http://dev.mysql.com/doc/mysql/en/show-create-procedure.html

Question 87: Stored Procedures Location

Where are Stored Procedures located?

A: Stored procedures are found in the proc table in the MySQL system database. However, you should not access the tables in the system database directly. Instead, use "SHOW CREATE [FUNCTION|PROCEDURE]." See the following link.

http://dev.mysql.com/doc/mysql/en/show-create-procedure.html)

Or INFORMATION_SCHEMA. See the following link.

http://dev.mysql.com/doc/mysql/en/routines-table.html

Question 88: Grouping Stored Procedures

Is it possible to group Stored Procedures into a package like Oracle for example?

A: No, not at present.

Question 89: Stored Procedure Calling another Stored Procedure/Trigger

Can a Stored Procedure call another Stored Procedure? How about a Trigger?

A: Yes and yes. A Stored Procedure can call another Stored Procedure and a Stored Procedure can also call a Trigger.

A stored procedure could execute an SQL statement (such as an UPDATE) that causes a trigger to fire.

Question 90: Stored Procedure Accessing Tables

Can Stored Procedures access a single Table? Multiple Tables?

A: Yes. Stored Procedures can access both single table and multiple tables.

Question 91: Stored Procedures' "Raise" Statement

Do Stored Procedures have a "raise" statement to "raise application errors"?

A: Sorry, not at present. The SQL standard "SIGNAL" and "RESIGNAL" statements are on the "TODO."

Question 92: Stored Procedures have Exception Handling

Do Stored Procedures have Exception Handling?

A: MySQL implements HANDLER definitions according to the SQL standard. See the link below for details.

http://dev.mysql.com/doc/mysql/en/declare-handlers.html

Question 93: Stored Procedures Return Result Sets

Can Stored Procedures return result sets (like MS SQL and Sybase)?

A: Yes. If you do an ordinary SELECT inside a stored procedure or function, the result set is returned directly to the client. You will need to use the MySQL 4.1 client-server protocol for this to work. This means that, for instance in PHP, you need to use the mysqli extension rather than the old mysql extension.

Question 94: "WITH RECOMPILE" for Stored Procedures

Can I do a "WITH RECOMPILE" for Stored Procedures?

A: For now, you can't do a "WITH RECOMPILE" for Stored Procedures.

Question 95: MySQL Equivalent of Oracle's Use of mod_plsql

Oracle uses "mod_plsql" as a gateway on Apache to talk directly to a Stored Procedure in the database. What is the MySQL equivalent?

A: There is no equivalent at present. Implementation of this should not be too difficult.

Question 96: Pass an Array as Input to a Stored Procedure

Can I pass an array as input to a Stored Procedure?

A: No, you can't pass an array as input to a Stored Procedure.

Question 97: Pass a Cursor as an IN Parameter to a Stored Procedure

Can I pass a cursor as an IN parameter to a Stored Procedure?

A: No. Currently, cursors are only available inside stored procedures.

Question 98: Cursor as an OUT parameter from a Stored Procedure

Can I return a cursor as an OUT parameter from a Stored Procedure?

A: No. Currently, cursors are only available inside stored procedures. However, you can return a result set from a SELECT by not opening a cursor on it (it will be sent directly to the client), or by selecting into variables.

Question 99: Print out a Variable Value in a Stored Procedure for Debugging

Can I print out a variable value in a Stored Procedure for debugging?

A: Yes. If you do an ordinary SELECT inside a stored procedure or function, the result set is returned directly to the client. You will need to use the MySQL 4.1 client-server protocol for this to work. This means that, for instance in PHP, you need to use the mysqli extension rather than the old mysql extension.

Question 100: Transaction inside a Stored Procedure

Can I do a "Transaction" inside a Stored Procedure (i.e., committing or rolling back a set of SQL statements in a batch)?

A: No, you can't do a "Transaction" inside a Stored Procedure.

Question 101: Documentation and Forums for MySQL Triggers

Where can I find documentation and forums for MySQL Triggers?

A: You can find documentation for MySQL Triggers in the MySQL Reference Manual accessible at:

http://dev.mysql.com/doc/mysql/en/show-create-procedure.html

The discussion forum for MySQL Triggers are found at:

http://forums.mysql.com/list.php?99

Question 102: Statement-level Triggers and Row-level Triggers

Do you have Statement-level Triggers or Row-level Triggers?

A: All triggers are "FOR EACH ROW," that is, the trigger is activated for each row that is inserted/updated/deleted. We currently don't allow "FOR EACH STATEMENT" triggers.

Question 103: Default Triggers

Are there any default Triggers?

A: Not explicitly. MySQL does have specific special behavior for some "TIMESTAMP" columns, and columns defined as "AUTO_INCREMENT."

Question 104: Managing Triggers

How do you manage Triggers?

A: A trigger can be created with a "CREATE TRIGGER" statement. See this link for details:

http://dev.mysql.com/doc/mysql/en/triggers.html

Management features, for instance, "INFORMATION_SCHEMA" are currently being implemented.

Question 105: View all Triggers in a Database

Is there a way to view all Triggers in a Database?

A: Yes, using the "INFORMATION_SCHEMA.TRIGGERS" table:

```
SELECT
TRIGGER_NAME,EVENT_MANIPULATION,EVENT_OBJECT_T
ABLE,ACTION_STATEMENT FROM
INFORMATION_SCHEMA.TRIGGERS WHERE
TRIGGER_SCHEMA='dbname'
```

See the link below:

http://dev.mysql.com/doc/mysql/en/triggers-table.html

You can also use the MySQL specific "SHOW TRIGGERS" statement. See the link at:

http://dev.mysql.com/doc/mysql/en/show-create-triggers.html

Question 106: Triggers Storage

Where are Triggers stored?

A: Currently, Triggers are stored individually for each table in a .TRG file, next to the normal ".FRM file" with the "CREATE TABLE" information. In the near future, the trigger information will be included in the ".FRM structure." In a nutshell, triggers belong with a table.

Work is currently being done to make triggers 'database level' objects (as opposed to 'table level' as they are now and mentioned above) as prescribed by the SQL standard.

Question 107: Trigger Calling a Stored Procedure

Can a Trigger call a Stored Procedure?

A: Yes, a Trigger can call a Stored Procedure.

Question 108: Triggers Accessing a Single/Multiple Tables

Can Triggers access a single Table? How about multiple Tables?

A: Yes. A Trigger can access information in its own table, both the old and the new data. Through a stored procedure or a multi-table update or delete statement, a Trigger can also affect multiple other tables.

Question 109: Triggers Calling an External Application

Can Triggers call an external application (through a UDF)?

A: At present, Triggers can not call an external application (through a UDF).

Question 110: Trigger Updating Tables on Remote Servers

Is there an example of a Trigger updating tables on remote servers?

A: Yes, a table on a remote server could be updated through the "FEDERATED storage engine." See the link below for more details.

http://dev.mysql.com/doc/mysql/en/federated-storage-engine.html

Question 111: Documentation and Discussion Forum for MySQL Views

Where can I find documentation and the discussion forum for MySQL Views?

A: You can find the documentation for MySQL Views in the "MySQL Reference Manual." The manual is at:

http://dev.mysql.com/doc/mysql/en/views.html

The discussion forum for MySQL Views can be found at:

http://forums.mysql.com/list.php?100

Question 112: Underlying Table is dropped

What happens if an underlying Table is dropped, renamed, etc.?

A: After a view has been created, it is possible to drop or alter a table or view to which the definition refers. To check a view definition for problems of this kind, use the "CHECK TABLE" statement.

Question 113: MySQL 5.0 Table Snapshots

Does MySQL 5.0 have "Table Snapshots"?

A: Sorry, MySQL 5.0 does not have "Table Snapshots."

Question 114: MySQL 5.0 Materialized Views

Does MySQL 5.0 have "Materialized Views"?

A: No. MySQL 5.0 does not have "Materialized Views."

Question 115: Insert into Views Based on Joins

Can you insert into Views based on Joins?

A: It is possible, provided that your "INSERT" statement has a column list that makes it clear there's only one table involved. You cannot insert into multiple tables with a single statement.

Question 116: Updating a View Affecting Multiple/Single table

Can updating a View affect multiple tables or single table?

A: Updating a View can affect only a single table.

Question 117: Documentation and Discussion Forum for MySQL INFORMATION_SCHEMA

Where can I find documentation and the discussion forum for MySQL INFORMATION_SCHEMA?

A: You can find documentation for MySQL INFORMATION_SCHEMA in the "MySQL Reference Manual" that can be found at:

http://dev.mysql.com/doc/mysql/en/information-schema-tables.html

The discussion forum for MySQL INFORMATION_SCHEMA can be found at:

http://forums.mysql.com/list.php?101

Question 118: ANSI SQL 2003 Specification for INFORMATION_SCHEMA

Where can I find the "ANSI SQL 2003 Specification" for INFORMATION_SCHEMA?

A: Unfortunately, the official specifications are not freely available. ANSI does make them available for purchase. However, there are books available, such as *SQL-99 Complete, Really* by Peter Gulutzan and Trudy Pelzer, which give a comprehensive overview of the standard including INFORMATION_SCHEMA.

Question 119: Difference between the Oracle Data Dictionary and MySQL INFORMATION_SCHEMA

What is the difference between the "Oracle Data Dictionary" and MySQL INFORMATION_SCHEMA?

A: At the overview level, there is no difference. Both Oracle and MySQL provide metadata information in tables. But at the detail level, there are many differences because Oracle and MySQL use different table names and column names for that metadata information. There is more similarity with DB2 and SQL Server, which also has an INFORMATION_SCHEMA as in the SQL standard.

Question 120: Groups of Tables in MySQL

Can I organize groups of Tables in MySQL (e.g., PostgreSQL does this with SCHEMA)?

A: Groups of tables are organized in a database. In most cases with MySQL, you can regard a database as equivalent to a schema.

Question 121: Tables in the INFORMATION_SCHEMA

Can I add or modify the Tables in the INFORMATION_SCHEMA?

A: No. Applications may rely on a certain standard structure, this should not be modified.

Question 122: MySQL Connector/J and the New Features in MySQL 5.0

Does MySQL Connector/J work with the new features in MySQL 5.0?

A: Only partially. Although version 3.51 does not support stored procedure calls using escape syntax (i.e., "{ call (...)}", or the server-side stored procedures, version 3.53, which is currently in development, will.

The JDBC forum is at

http://forums.mysql.com/list.php?39

Question 123: MySQL Connector/NET and the New Features in MySQL 5.0

Does MySQL Connector/NET work with the new features in MySQL 5.0?

A: Yes, the MySQL Connector/NET works with the new features in MySQL 5.0.

The .Net forum is at:

http://forums.mysql.com/list.php?38

Question 124: MySQL Connector/ODBC and the New Features in MySQL 5.0

Does MySQL Connector/ODBC work with the new features in MySQL 5.0?

A: Yes, MySQL Connector/ODBC works with the new features in MySQL 5.0.

The ODBC forum is at:

http://forums.mysql.com/list.php?37

Question 125: DBD: MySQL and the New Features in MySQL 5.0

Does DBD::MySQL (the Perl MySQL driver) work with the new features in MySQL 5.0?

A: Yes, DBD::MySQL (the Perl MySQL driver) works with the new features in MySQL 5.0.

The Perl forum is at:

http://forums.mysql.com/list.php?51

Question 126: MySQL and MySQLI extensions and the New Features in MySQL 5.0

Do the MySQL and MySQLI extensions (the PHP MySQL APIs) work with the new features in MySQL 5.0?

A: The old MySQL extension can work with MySQL 5.0, but does not support the new authentication protocol (MySQL 4.1), prepared statements (MySQL 4.1), cursors, or multiple result sets. Only the new MySQLI extension (PHP 5.0 and up) covers and supports all features of MySQL 4.1 and 5.0.

The PHP forum is at:

http://forums.mysql.com/list.php?52

Question 127: Instance Manager Enable Management of Remote MySQL Servers

Can Instance Manager enable management of remote MySQL servers?

A: Yes. Please see the link below for more information about the "MySQL Instance Manager."

http://dev.mysql.com/doc/mysql/en/instance-manager.html

Question 128: Instance Manager on a Windows Machine

Can you run Instance Manager on a Windows machine to manage MySQL on remote Linux machines?

A: "MySQL Instance Manager" is currently only available for Unix-like operating systems. This precludes Windows. A Windows version is under active development and should be available shortly.

Question 129: GUI Tools Availability on Linux

Are GUI (Graphical User Interface) Tools available on Linux?

A: The following MySQL GUI Tools are available for download: "MySQL Administrator" (for DBA tasks), "MySQL Query Browser" (for developers). More "MySQL GUI Tools" are under development, as well as continued enhancements to the existing tools. See the following links for details on each of these tools.

http://www.mysql.com/products/administrator/

http://www.mysql.com/products/query-browser/

The MySQL Administrator forum is at:

http://forums.mysql.com/list.php?34

The MySQL Query browser forum is at:

http://forums.mysql.com/list.php?108

Question 130: MySQL Administrator and the New Features in MySQL 5.0

Can MySQL Administrator work with the new features in MySQL 5.0?

A: Yes, the MySQL Administrator works with the new features in MySQL 5.0.

Question 131: MySQL Query Browser and the New Features in MySQL 5.0

Can MySQL Query Browser work with the new features in MySQL 5.0?

A: Yes, MySQL Query Browser works with the new features in MySQL 5.0.

Question 132: MySQL GUI Tools to Build Stored Procedures and Views

Can you use MySQL GUI Tools to build Stored Procedures and Views?

A: Yes, you can use MySQL GUI Tools to build Stored Procedures and Views. Additional GUI Tool features to ease development and debugging of Stored Procedures, etc. are under development. The GUI Tools have a higher release frequency and versions with new features and fixes are released frequently.

Question 133: Backup/Restore and mysqldump Work with Stored Procedures

When will Backup/Restore and mysqldump work with Stored Procedures?

A: As of the production release of MySQL 5.0, Backup/Restore and mysqldump will backup and restore Stored Procedures.

Question 134: Mysqldump Actually Dump the Definitions of Stored Procedures, Triggers, and Functions

When will mysqldump actually dump the definitions of Stored Procedures, Triggers, and Functions?

A: As of the production release of MySQL 5.0, mysqldump dumps Stored Procedures, Triggers, and Functions.

Question 135: Migrate from MySQL 4.x to 5.0

How do you migrate from MySQL 4.x to 5.0?

A: Detailed upgrade information for each version can be found at:

http://dev.mysql.com/doc/mysql/en/upgrade.html.

We recommend that you do not skip a major version when upgrading, but rather upgrade in steps (for instance, if you are still using MySQL 4.0 but wish to upgrade to 5.0, upgrade your (test) system to 4.1 first, and verify that everything is as it should be. Then proceed with the 4.1 to 5.0 upgrade step). This may seem more complicated, but it will probably save you time and hassle—if you find any problems along the way, their origin will be easier to identify (either by you or MySQL support, if you have a MySQL Network subscription).

Question 136: Table Types Change

Have the Table Types changed from MySQL 4.x to 5.0?

A: Support for the old ISAM tables (used until MySQL 3.22) was removed in MySQL 5.0. To convert a table from ISAM to MyISAM, simply issue a statement like ALTER TABLE tblname ENGINE=MYISAM.

The "internal RAID" support in MyISAM tables was also removed. This was an old feature used to allow large tables with file systems that did not support large (>2GB) files. All modern file systems allow for larger tables and there are also other solutions such as MERGE tables and VIEWs.

The VARCHAR column type now retains any trailing spaces (all storage engines).

MEMORY tables (called HEAP, prior to MySQL version 4.1) can now also contain VARCHAR columns.

Question 137: MySQL 5.0 Support for SSL

Does MySQL 5.0 have native support for SSL?

A: Yes, most MySQL 5.0 binaries have support for SSL secured and/or authenticated connections between the client and server. We can't currently build with the new YaSSL library everywhere, as it's still quite new and does not compile on all platforms yet. See the following site:

http://dev.mysql.com/doc/mysql/en/secure-connections.html

You could also tunnel the connection via SSH, for instance if the client application doesn't support SSL connections. For an example of this, see:

http://dev.mysql.com/doc/mysql/en/windows-and-ssh.html

Question 138: SSL Support for the MySQL Binaries

Will the SSL Support be built into the MySQL Binaries or will it require a recompile?

A: Most MySQL 5.0 binaries have SSL enabled for secured and/or authenticated connections between the client and server. We can't currently build with the new "YaSSL library" everywhere as it's still quite new and does not compile on all platforms yet. See the website below for details:

http://dev.mysql.com/doc/mysql/en/secure-connections.html

Question 139: MySQL 5.0 Built-in Authentication against LDAP Directories

Does MySQL 5.0 have built-in Authentication against LDAP directories?

A: No. Support for external authentication methods is on the MySQL roadmap as a "rolling feature." This means that it is not a flagship feature, but will be implemented, development time permitting. Specific customer demand may change this scheduling.

Question 140: MySQL 5.0 Built-in Roles Based Access Control (RBAC)

Does MySQL 5.0 have built-in Roles Based Access Control (RBAC)?

A: No. Roles are on the MySQL roadmap as a "rolling feature." This means that it is not a flagship feature, but will be implemented, development time permitting. Specific customer demand may change this scheduling.

Question 141: Benefits for an ISV/VAR to Embed MySQL into a Software or Hardware System

What are the benefits for an ISV/VAR to embed MySQL into a software or hardware system?

A: By embedding MySQL, an ISV/VAR delivers the following benefits to the customer:

> Deliver a complete solution to the customer. Eliminate the need for the customer to evaluate, buy, and implement a separate database.

> Reduce the time required to "go live" for the customer. Eliminate the time required for development and testing cycles to implement a new database.

> Reduce the total cost of ownership (TCO) for the customer. MySQL reduces database licensing costs by over 90% and cuts system downtime by 60%.

By embedding MySQL, an ISV/VAR can focus on its core business:

> Focus your core engineers on your product. By embedding MySQL, your engineers do not have to build and maintain a proprietary database.

> Win competitive comparisons. MySQL is recognized for superior performance and reliability.

> Increase your revenue margin. Lower the cost of your solution by embedding MySQL, the low-cost database leader, available with flexible licensing terms.

> Keep a bigger share of the customer's budget.
Embedding MySQL eliminates the need for the customer
to purchase a separate database.

Question 142: Scenarios for Embedding MySQL

What are the scenarios for embedding MySQL?

A: There are 2 scenarios for embedding MySQL.

Scenario 1: Deeply Embedded MySQL

The customer has no visibility into the operation of the
database. The ISV/VAR is using the embedded MySQL
Server Library (libmysqld) as an in-process data storage
engine that provides all the features of a traditional
relational database but in a size which makes it useable for
application and hardware designers who need a small
footprint and need a simple and easy to use toolkit.

For example, S2 Security has developed a physical security
appliance called the S2 Netbox which embeds MySQL in
ROM running on an embedded version of Linux. S2
Netbox provides a highly configurable integrated security
system featuring access control, alarm monitoring, video
surveillance, and a range of other applications. By
embedding MySQL they are able to provide a highly
sophisticated reporting system that is easy to use and gives
them the scalability and performance they need for
demanding enterprise customers.

Scenario 2: Bundled MySQL

The customer has complete visibility and control over the
database, enabling them to configure, tune, optimize, and
administer the database. The ISV/VAR uses the MySQL
Server as a standalone relational database.

For example, Sterling Commerce's popular Gentran Integration Suite is used by Global 5000 customers as a messaging gateway for Business-to-Business, EDI, and EAI. By shipping MySQL as a bundled database, Sterling Commerce customers can reduce their TCO by not having to separately budget for and purchase a database. Customers have the ability to configure, tune, and administer the MySQL database for optimum performance of the Gentran application.

Question 143: Key Relational Database Features that MySQL Provides

What are the key Relational Database features that MySQL provides?

A: MySQL supports all the key Relational Database features, including:

> High-performance.

> Main-memory and disk-based tables.

> Single-User and Multi-User.

> Multi-Threaded.

> SQL-92 and SQL-99.

> ACID Transactions.

> Referential Integrity.

> Cascading Updates and Deletes.

> Multi-table Joins.

> Row-level Locking.

> Replication.

> Clustering.

> BLOBs (Binary Large Objects).

> UDFs (User Defined Functions).

> OLTP (On-Line Transaction Processing).

> Unicode and Double-Byte character support.

> Drivers for ODBC, JDBC, .NET and C++.

Question 144: Synchronization and Replication Capabilities of MySQL

What are the Synchronization and Replication capabilities of MySQL?

A: Synchronization is a "required" when an organization has:

> Remote systems, which need real-time or periodic updates (e.g., a bank teller machine).

> Mobile users, who typically need occasional updates (e.g., a traveling sales person).

MySQL provides synchronization via its Master-Slave Replication capabilities. Extensive documentation makes it easy to setup and configure MySQL for replication.

Question 145: Performance and Scalability Characteristics of MySQL

What are the Performance and Scalability characteristics of MySQL?

A: In February 2002, eWeek published the results of their Database Benchmark Test, showing:

> MySQL has the best overall performance and scalability (matching Oracle).

> MySQL excelled in stability, ease of tuning, and connectivity.

> MySQL offered the highest throughput (600 web pages/sec to 1000 concurrent users).

> MySQL's performance advantage came from a unique feature - the ability to use different database engines on a table-by-table basis.

See the link below to view the results of eWeek Database Benchmark test:

http://www.mysql.com/why-mysql/benchmarks/

Question 146: MySQL Reliability

How Reliable is MySQL?

A: MySQL has a well-earned and established reputation for reliability and performance among its 6 million user community. MySQL is embedded by leading companies including Cisco, Ericsson, Motorola, NEC, Novell, and Symantec.

In December 2003, Reasoning published the results of their Code Quality Inspection Study of MySQL, showing:

> MySQL code quality was 6x better than that of comparable proprietary code.

> MySQL benefits from the large communities of programmers who "battle test" the code.

> MySQL benefits from users who not only report bugs, but track down their root cause and fix them.

See the link below to view the results of Reasoning's Code Quality Analysis of MySQL.

http://www.mysql.com/why-mysql/quality/

Question 147: MySQL Easy to Administer

Is MySQL easy to Administer?

A: MySQL has a well-earned and established reputation as an easy-to-administer database. Developers have the flexibility to configure, tune, and optimize MySQL. Users typically are unaware of the existence of the database and do not need a database administrator, since the install takes care of the configuration.

Question 148: Minimum System Requirements for MySQL

What are the minimum system requirements for MySQL?

A: The minimum system requirements for MySQL are as follows:

> Minimum memory: 1 MB of RAM.

> Minimum disk-based server: 4 MB of Hard Disk.

> Default disk-based server: 8 MB of Hard Disk.

Question 149: Platforms MySQL Support

What Platforms does MySQL support?

A: MySQL runs on:

> Linux (RedHat, SuSE, Mandrake, Debian).

> Embedded Linux (MontaVista, LynuxWorks BlueCat).

> Unix (Solaris, HP-UX, AIX).

> BSD (Mac OS X, FreeBSD).

> Windows (Windows 2000, Windows NT, Windows XP).

> RTOS (QNX).

> Handheld (Windows CE).

Question 150: Industry Standards and 3rd Party Tools MySQL Support

What industry standards and 3rd party tools does MySQL support?

A: MySQL has drivers for:

> ODBC

> JDBC

> .NET

> C++

MySQL application can be developed in any popular language, including:

> C

> C++

> C#

> Java

> Delphi

> Visual Basic

> Perl

> Python

> PHP

MySQL applications can be developed using popular Development Tools, including:

> Microsoft Visual Studio

> Borland Delphi and JBuilder

> Eclipse

> NetBeans

MySQL databases can be administered using popular Database Tools, including:

> MySQL Administrator

> Quest Software Toad for MySQL

> Embarcadero ER/Studio

MySQL applications can be deployed using popular Deployment Tools, including:

> InstallShield

> WiseInstaller

Question 151: MySQL Reduce TCO

How does MySQL reduce TCO?

A: MySQL reduces the Total Cost of Ownership (TCO) of database software by:

> Reducing database licensing costs by over 90%

> Cutting systems downtime by 60%

> Lowering hardware expenditure by 70%

> Reducing administration, engineering, and support costs by up to 50%

For more information, read the white paper "A Guide to Lower Database TCO" found at:

http://www.mysql.com/why-mysql/white-papers/tco.php

Question 152: Pricing Model for Embedding MySQL

What is the pricing model for embedding MySQL?

A: MySQL is flexible and will work with you to identify intelligent pricing models based on:

> Buying MySQL licenses at a discount off MySQL list price.

> Royalties on a percentage of your applications published list price.

For pricing details, please call 425-743-5635 or contact us online at:

http://www.mysql.com/company/contact/

Question 153: ISV/VARs that currently embed MySQL

Which ISV/VARs currently embed MySQL?

A: MySQL is deployed to over 8 million active users.

ISV/VARs who have embedded MySQL, include:

> Telecom: Agilent, Alcatel, Cisco, Ericsson, F5 Networks, Motorola, NEC, SS8 Networks.

> Retail: The Gap, Suzuki Kiosks.

> BioTech: Biotique Systems.

> ISV: Network Associates, Novell, Quest Software, Symantec.

Question 154: Partner Program for Companies Interested in Embedding MySQL

Is there a "Partner Program" for companies interested in embedding MySQL?

A: Yes, there is a "Partner Program" for companies interested in embedding MySQL. For more information, visit the website below:

http://solutions.mysql.com/program/

Question 155: Information about Embedding MySQL

Where can I get more information about embedding MySQL?

A: You can get more information about embedding MySQL at the following links:

http://www.mysql.com/oem/index.html

http://dev.mysql.com/doc/refman/5.0/en/libmysqld-overview.html

Question 156: Primary Business Benefit that MySQL Provides

What is the primary business benefit that MySQL provides?

A: MySQL is a proven and cost-effective database solution that will help reduce the cost of your database software infrastructure by over 90%.
For more information, read the white paper "A Guide to Lower Database TCO" at:

http://www.mysql.com/tco/

Question 157: Additional Benefits MySQL Provide

What additional benefits does MySQL provide?

A: Listed below are the additional benefits that MySQL provides.

> Easy to Install and Deploy: Users can set up MySQL in minutes enabling organizations to deliver new applications faster than with proprietary databases.

> Easy to Administer: MySQL is a low administration database that eliminates the need for highly trained, skilled, and costly database administrators to maintain the database.

> High Performance: In February 2002, eWeek published the results of their Database Benchmark Test, showing MySQL has the best overall performance and scalability

(matching Oracle). To view the results of eWeek Database Benchmark test visit the link at:

http://www.mysql.com/benchmarks/

> Reliability and High Availability: MySQL has a well-earned and established reputation for reliability among its 5 million user community. In addition to reliability, MySQL Cluster provides 99.999% availability.

> Embeddable Library: The embedded MySQL Server Library (lib mysqld) provides in-process data storage engine that delivers all the features of a traditional relational database but in a size which makes it ideally suited for ISVs/VARs who need a small footprint and easy to use toolkit.

> Platform Independence: MySQL runs on over 20 platforms including Linux, Solaris, AIX, HP-UX, Windows, and Mac OS X giving organizations complete flexibility in delivering a solution on the platform of their choice.

Question 158: MySQL Support ISV/VARs Who Want to Distribute MySQL

How does MySQL support ISV/VARs who want to distribute MySQL as part of their solution?

A: MySQL support ISV/VARs who want to distribute MySQL as part of their solution by the following possibilities.

Scenario 1: Deeply Embedded MySQL

The customer has no visibility into the operation of the database. The ISV/VAR is using the embedded MySQL

Server Library (libmysqld) as an in-process data storage engine that provides all the features of a traditional relational database but in a size which makes it useable for application and hardware designers who need a small footprint and need a simple and easy to use toolkit.

Scenario 2: Bundled MySQL

The customer has complete visibility and control over the database, enabling them to configure, tune, optimize, and administer the database. The ISV/VAR uses the MySQL Server as a standalone relational database.

Question 159: Installed Base of MySQL

What is the Installed Base of MySQL?

A: MySQL has an active installed base of 5 million users, with over 35,000 daily downloads.

In a July 2004 article, SD Times shows MySQL as the #3 most deployed database. With 33% market-share, MySQL is more widely deployed than Sybase or DB2. See the link below for more details.

http://www.mysql.com/marketshare/

Question 160: Customer References for MySQL

Where can I find Customer References for MySQL?

A: MySQL customers include Global 2000 organizations such as Alcatel, Apple, Associated Press, Bloomberg, BMC, CERN, Cisco, Ericsson, Google, Lufthansa, Motorola, NASA, NEC, Netflix, Nokia, Nortel, Sabre, SAS, and many more.

For case studies and articles, see:

http://www.mysql.com/customers/

Question 161: Fully Supported

What is Fully Supported (FS)?

A: These are operating system and hardware combinations which are primary platforms for MySQL usage. MySQL builds and tests binaries for these combinations using our own hardware. All forms of MySQL binaries can be included under this tier: Certified, Production (GA), Alpha, Beta, and Gamma. There should be no technical scenarios on these platforms which the MySQL Support Team cannot resolve to a reasonable level.

Question 162: Conditionally Supported

What is Conditionally Supported (CS)?

A: These are operating system and hardware combinations for which MySQL provides conditional support. For this tier, MySQL may not have the target OS/hardware, MySQL may have documented issues, or the OS and/or hardware vendors may not be actively supporting their platform components. The MySQL Support Team will attempt to provide technical support for these platforms, but with the customer's acknowledgement that there may be scenarios that cannot be resolved.

Question 163: Limited Support

What is Limited Support (LS)?

A: These are specific operating system and hardware combinations for which MySQL provides only limited support. For this tier, MySQL does not have the target OS/hardware, MySQL does not build binaries for these combinations, and MySQL does not test on these platforms. The MySQL Support Team will use commercially reasonable efforts to attempt to provide technical support for these platforms, but with the customer's acknowledgement that there may be scenarios that cannot be resolved due to the above limitations.

Question 164: Who uses MySQL?

MySQL is very useful, but who really uses MySQL?

A: Yes, it is very useful and more and more companies are signing up for this product. For instance:

BioPharma

- BASE: BioArray Software Environment
- Bayer
- Center for Biological Sequence Analysis (CBS)
- Colgate
- Ensembl Genome Browser
- EraGen Biosciences
- Genome Sciences Center (GSC)
- Sanger Institute
- The Institute for Genomic Research

Defense

- AIRBUS/EADS
- Defense Technical Information Center (DTIC)
- EUROCOPTER
- French Ministry of Defense
- Los Alamos National Laboratory
- Thales Avionics

e-Commerce

- Charlwood eMarketing
- CitySearch
- ClassMates
- CraigsList
- eFashion
- Evite
- Friend Finder Network

- Google
- Hot or Not
- hotpads.com
- iStockphoto
- LiveWorld
- Lycos Europe
- MyPoints
- Powell's books
- PriceGrabber
- Spray
- Ticketmaster
- WebTrends
- Yahoo!

Education

- American Education Corporation
- AUF (Agence Universitaire de la Francophonie)
- CERN - The ATLAS Experiment at LHC
- LeapFrog SchoolHouse
- MIT Lincoln Lab
- Red Deer College
- University of California, Berkeley
- University of Texas

Energy

- ENERCON
- Fortum
- Fuel Cells 2000
- Pason Systems Inc.
- Schlumberger Industries

Finance

- Aizawa-Securities Ltd.
- APRIL GROUP

- Bank of Canada
- Boursorama
- Chicago Mercantile Exchange
- HypoVereinsbank
- Lloyds TSB Bank
- Nürnberger Versicherungsgruppe
- Securities America

Gaming

- Greyhound-Data
- Habbo Hotel
- Linden Lab (Second Life)
- Mythic Entertainment (Dark Age of Camelot)
- Neopets
- Ongame (PokerRoom.com)
- PROTRADE
- SimDynasty
- Tomb Raider Chronicles

Government

- ADEME
- Australian Sports Commission
- California Air Review Board
- City of New York
- CNES (Centre National d'Etudes Spatiales)
- CNRS (Centre National de la Recherche Scientifique)
- Department of Homeland Security
- Deutsche Post
- Government Open Code Collaborative (GOCC)
- IRSN (Institut de Radioproctection et de Surete Nucleaire)
- NASA
- NASA Jet Propulsion Lab (JPL)
- Pottawattamie County
- RATP
- State of Illinois

- State of Michigan
- State of Minnesota
- State of New York
- State of Parana
- State of Rhode Island
- U.S. Census Bureau
- United Nations FAO

Healthcare

- CanadaDrugs
- Cardinal Health
- Finnish National Public Health Institute
- InsiteOne
- Institut Curie
- Médecins Sans Frontières (Doctors Without Borders)
- Swisslog
- UNICEF
- Westone Laboratories, Inc.

Manufacturing

- Avery Dennison
- Braun
- DaimlerChrysler
- Epson
- Hillerich & Bradsby (Louisville Slugger)
- Smurfit-Stone
- Toyota France
- Toyota South Africa
- WS Atkins PLC
- Yamaha

Media

- AlwaysOn Network

- Associated Press
- BBC News
- Bloomberg L.P.
- Chicago Sun-Times
- Christian Science Monitor
- CNET Networks
- DirecTV
- Eniro
- EurotaxGlass Schweiz AG
- Hoover's
- IDG.se
- Mainstream Advertising
- MetService
- Nine Systems
- SBS (Australia)
- Seat Pagine Gialle
- Slashdot
- The Leaky Cauldron (Webby Award Winner)
- The Weather Channel (Weather.com)

Open Source Projects

- eGroupWare
- Fedora Project
- LAMP (Linux/Apache/MySQL/Perl/PHP/Python)
- OpenOffice
- osCommerce
- PHP-Nuke
- phpBB
- PHProjekt
- PostNuke
- Snort
- SugarCRM
- WAMP
  (Windows/Apache/MySQL/Perl/PHP/Python)
- XOOPS

Retail

- Axfood AB
- Braintree Sourcing (Stop & Shop)
- De La Rue
- Donut King
- Franprix
- H&M Rowells
- Leader Price
- Macy's West
- neckermann.de
- Omaha Steaks
- SAGEM Monetel
- Suzuki
- The Spirit Group
- Yves Rocher

Technology

- Agilent
- Agilent Technologies
- Apple
- BMC
- Cap Gemini Ernst & Young
- Dell
- eZ Systems
- Hewlett-Packard
- Hyperion
- Intel
- Matra Grolier Network
- McAfee
- Mediapps SA
- Motorola
- NEC
- NetIQ
- NetQoS
- Novell
- Omniture

- Proofpoint
- Quest Software
- RightNow Technologies
- RLX Technologies
- Roland Messerli AG
- S2 Security Corporation
- Sandstorm Enterprises
- SAS
- Sega Europe Ltd
- Somix
- Sony Deutschland GmbH
- Standard Networks
- Sterling Commerce
- Sun Microsystems
- Symantec
- Texas Instruments
- Veritas
- Xerox Research Centre Europe

Telecom

- 3COM
- 8x8, Inc.
- Active Voice
- Alcatel
- AT&T Wireless
- Bredbandsbolaget (B2)
- British Telecommunications plc
- Cable & Wireless
- Cisco Systems
- Cox Communications
- EarthLink
- Ericsson
- F5 Networks
- France Telecom
- handy.de
- Lucent
- Matanuska Telephone Association (MTA)
- Nokia

- Nortel Networks
- Onlinetel Corp.
- PortaOne
- Siemens
- SS8 Networks
- T-Systems International
- Tekelec
- Telio
- Tellme Networks
- UTEL
- Vocera

Transport

- AXS Marine
- Canadian Civil Air Search and Rescue Association (CASARA)
- GHY International
- Owens Cargo Company Ltd.
- Red One Aviation
- UPS
- Viasuisse

Travel

- Continental Airlines
- Farecast
- lastminute.com
- Lufthansa Systems
- Orbitz
- Pivex
- Sabre Holdings

Web 2.0

- 37signals
- Cyworld

- del.icio.us
- Digg
- Eventfinder
- Facebook
- Feedburner
- Feedster
- Flickr
- Freshmeat.net
- Friendster
- Jigsaw
- LiveJournal
- Mixi.jp
- Photobucket
- Simple Star PhotoShow
- Technorati
- Trulia
- Wikipedia
- YouTube

Useful Links and Sites

http://www.mysql.com

Index

"InnoDB Hot-Backup"? .. 66
"internal RAID" support105
"native" language............ 11
"rolling feature"............. 65
"Server SQL Mode"........ 69
"SQL-99 Complete, Really"
................................73
"Strict Mode" Impact 71
(DTP) support................14
'--initial startup' option...53
".tar.gz" archives............ 50
"AUTO_INCREMENT"
system 64
"CHECK TABLE" statement
..................................91
"five nines" availability... 60
"hot" reconfiguration......53
"majority rules" situation58
"MySQL Reference Manual"
................................72
"SHOW TRIGGERS"
statement.................. 86
100-megabit Ethernet
network 43
255 characters.............. 59
3.23-Max 67
3rd Party Tools............. 118
70 questions..................35
90 minutes...................35
account node groups 58
ACID compliance............15
ACID Transactions....67, 111
active installed base......126
Add Nodes 53
addendum..................... 30
Additional Benefits.......124
additional points of failure
.... 60
Administer 116
Administering MySQL 12
affected node................ 62

aligned.......................... 28
alpha stages.................. 62
alter..............................91
ANSI C.......................... 11
ANSI SQL 2003
specification...............73
ANSI SQL 2003
Specification............. 93
APIs.............................. 11
ArbitrationRank............ 59
Arbitrator...................... 58
ARCHIVE Storage Engine
.... 68
asynchronous............... 42
authenticated connections
................................106
authentication protocol.. 98
backport....................... 42
Backup/Restore and
mysqldump Work.....103
battle test 115
Benefits........................25
Benefits for an ISV/VAR to
Embed MySQL 109
Beta............................. 29
Beta exams....................37
binaries........................106
Binary Large Objects..... 112
BLOB values.................. 54
body of individual stored
procedures.................75
broad subset..................13
BSD 117
Build Stored Procedures 101
Bundled MySQL 110, 126
Calling 76
Capabilities 40
Catastrophic Failure....... 50
certain standard structure
.... 95
Certificate Copy.............37

Certification Exams
    Preparation...............27
certification exams?........27
character sets 54
chief reasons 51
clear naming scheme.......73
Closed Book Exams.........35
Cluster 42
cluster fail..................... 58
cluster hosts................. 60
cluster node processes.....53
Cluster Nodes
    Communication......... 56
collations 54
column type 68
Column-level constraints.16
command-line tool.........12
committed sequentially .. 42
committed transactions.. 50
Community Edition........18
Compatible.................... 11
compile......................... 49
complete columns.......... 54
complete result sets 64
complete solution.........109
complete visibility and
    control.....................126
Conditionally Supported129
configure..................... 116
Configuring Server SQL
    Mode........................ 70
continued arbitration
    services 44
Core certificiation.......... 32
core engineers 109
cost-effective.................124
created on-the-fly 37
Cross-platform support...13
current mode................. 70
Customer References 128
Data node..................... 45
data nodes..................... 44

Data Types supported 59
Database 64
Database Benchmark Test
    114
database component.......12
database software
    infrastructure 124
database solution.........124
DBA certifications.......... 32
DBAs............................25
DBD: MySQL................. 98
Debugging.....................81
decreased memory usage40
dedicated high-speed
    connectivity............... 46
Deeply Embedded MySQL
    .... 110, 126
default behaviour...........72
Default disk-based server
    116
default SQL mode.......... 70
Default Triggers............. 84
DELETE........................ 63
detailed information...... 38
detailed validation.......... 71
Details of Exam Result....37
Developer...................... 32
developers.....................25
development time
    permitting................ 65
DHCP 60
difference..................... 42
different clients 69
different environments... 69
Different kinds of hardware
    60
Disk-based MySQL Cluster
    40
Distinguishing Features .. 17
distribute MySQL 125
DNS............................. 60

Documentation and Forums
for MySQL Triggers ... 83
drop..............................91
dropping primary and
unique indexes 47
Dual Core Opterons 65
Duration 35
Dynamic Duo 12
Easy to Administer........124
Easy to Install and Deploy
................................124
easy-to-administer
database.................. 116
edge..............................25
embed MySQL.............. 121
Embeddable Library 125
Embedded database library
................................15
Embedded Linux 117
Embedding MySQL 121
ENGINE=NDBCLUSTER56
Error or Warning Message
.... 48
Error Reporting............. 66
escape syntax 95
Essential infrastructure.. 40
Event Scheduling............16
Exams Cost 39
Exception Handling....... 78
execute..........................76
Existing MySQL Database
.... 56
Extending "Strict Mode"
Rules 71
external authentication
methods...................108
extra debug information..18
extra studies..................37
Fail-safe replication........16
faster CPUs 46
faster SCI protocol......... 43
features.........................13

FEDERATED storage
engine........................67
fixed IP addresses.......... 60
flagship feature.........40, 65
flexibility..................... 116
FLOSS License Exception20
Foreign Key................... 66
Foreign key support........16
formal prerequisites....... 32
four 43
four SQL standard isolation
levels 67
fractional component..... 65
Fractions of Seconds...... 65
Full Unicode support......15
FULLTEXT Indexes with
Cluster 51
Full-text indexing 14
Fully Supported............128
functional cluster........... 58
Functionality 45
future release 51
General Availability 29
Gentran application.......111
global foreign key support
.... 66
GNU General Public License
.... 20
good practice.................73
Graphical User Interface100
Grouping Stored Procedures
................................76
Groups of Tables............ 95
GUI administration tools. 12
GUI Tools....................100
Handheld......................117
HANDLER definitions ... 78
Hardware Requirements 46
High Performance......... 125
high-availability protocol56
high-bandwidth
environment.............. 43
higher release frequency 101

highly configurable integrated security system 110
high-speed 56
Hostnames................... 60
Importing..................... 56
IN parameter.................81
individually switched on and off 69
Industry Standards....... 118
Information about Embedding MySQL ...123
INFORMATION_SCHEMA 14, 68
InnoDB storage engine... 17, 67
in-process data storage engine.......................126
input data 71
Insert into Views Based on Joins........................ 92
Installed Base of MySQL126
Instance........................ 64
Instance Manager 99
intended........................ 43
isolation levels.............. 48
ISV/VARs 121
Key Relational Database Features...................111
latest binary 50
latest MySQL certification developments............ 39
Latest MySQL Version....13
Length of Certification Validity 29
level of certification....... 33
lexer 18
limitation..................... 56
Limitations of using Cluster 54
limited.......................... 50
Limited Support 129

lingua franca................. 11
Linux 117
Linux users 50
logged........................... 50
logical organization........ 45
management and SQL nodes....................... 43
Management node 45
managing SQL nodes 47
Managing Stored Procedures 73
Managing Triggers......... 84
manual 35, 72
master 14
master MySQL server..... 42
Master-Slave Replication capabilities............... 113
Migrate from MySQL 4.x 104
minimum...................... 43
minimum connectivity requirements............. 43
Minimum disk-based server 116
Minimum memory........ 116
Minimum System Requirements........... 116
Mode Dependency 70
modify 95
multi-master replication setup......................... 64
multiple CPUs 65
multiple result sets......... 98
Multiple storage engines . 17
Multiple Tables...............77
Multi-table Inserts......... 63
Multi-table Joins 112
Multi-table UPDATE...... 63
multi-threaded......... 10, 65
multi-user 10
multi-versioning.............67
MyISAM.......................51

MyISAM for read speed...14
MyISAM Hot-Backup..... 66
MyODBC........................ 11
MySQL...........................10
MySQL 5.0 39
MySQL 5.0 "NOW()" 65
MySQL 5.0 a
    Production/GA 62
MySQL 5.0 Built-in
    Authentication against
    LDAP Directories......108
MySQL 5.0 Built-in Roles
    Based Access Control
    (RBAC) 108
MySQL 5.0 Materialized
    Views.........................91
MySQL 5.0 Sequences.... 64
MySQL 5.0 Subqueries... 63
MySQL 5.0 Support for SSL
   106
MySQL AB 10, 37
MySQL Administrator... 101
MySQL Binaries............106
MySQL Certification.......25
MySQL Certification
    Developments 39
MySQL Certification Levels
    26
MySQL Certification
    mailing list................ 39
MySQL Certification Study
    Guide........................ 30
MySQL certified user 25
MySQL client................ 48
MySQL Cluster......... 39, 45
MySQL Cluster
    Transaction-safe........ 48
MySQL Connector 97
MySQL Connector/J...... 95
MySQL Connector/ODBC97
MySQL Core Certification
    ....26, 33

MySQL Database
    Administrator
    Certification.............. 26
MySQL Default Mode......72
MySQL Developer...........25
MySQL Developer
    Certification.............. 26
MySQL Equivalent......... 80
MySQL Future Releases ..16
MySQL GUI Tools......... 101
MySQL
    INFORMATION_SCHE
    MA 92
My SQL Licensing........... 20
MySQL Platforms
    Compatibility 13
MySQL Professional
    Certification.............. 26
MySQL Query Browser.. 101
MySQL Query Cache 64
MySQL reduce TCO 120
MySQL Reliability......... 115
MySQL roadmap 65
MySQL Server Compilations
    17
MySQL server software .. 20
MySQL Source Code
    Specifics....................18
MySQL spatial extensions59
MySQL Stored Procedures
   72
MySQL support ISV/VARs
    125
MySQL Technical Support
   18
MySQL version 4.0 27
MySQL version 4.1 27
MySQL Versions.............27
MySQL Views 89
mysqld-max Extended
    MySQL Server............ 17
Mysqldump.................103
my sqli extensions 98

MySQL-max binaries 49
MySQL-Standard binaries17
native support 106
NDB storage engine .. 48, 49
NDB tables.................... 54
NDB-enabled binaries.... 46
network partitioning...... 58
New Features 40, 68
new MGM 53
No Negative Score...........35
no substitute 30
non-locking repeatable
    reads..........................67
not advisable 51
Number of Computers
    needed...................... 43
Number of Exams Needed
    32
Number of Modes 69
ODBC interface............... 11
official specifications...... 93
old ISAM tables............. 105
Online backup................ 16
on-line bookstores......... 28
On-Line Transaction
    Processing................. 112
operating systems.......... 60
optimize....................... 116
Oracle Data Dictionary... 93
Oracle's Use of mod_plsql
    80
ordinary SELECT...... 78, 81
organized...................... 95
original query string....... 64
OS in a Cluster............... 60
OUT parameter 81
overview level................ 93
particular database 70
Partitioning................... 16
Partner Program............123
pass............................. 33
Pass a Cursor.................81

Pass an Array as Input.... 80
Performance.............71, 114
periodic updates............ 113
Person VUE................... 30
physical elements 45
Platform Independence. 125
platforms 13
Platforms MySQL Support
   117
port 13
postal mail 37
precision math.............. 68
prepared statements 98
Prerequisites 32, 33
Pricing Model............... 121
Primary Business benefit
   124
proc table......................75
production version..........27
professional credentials...25
Professional exam.......... 32
programming languages.. 11
proprietary code........... 115
protective mechanism.....47
protocols...................... 56
proven 124
Query caching................ 14
query language...............47
Querying Cluster............47
raise application errors .. 78
RDBMSes...................... 17
real-time 113
recent versions 13
recompile.....................106
redundancy 44, 51
Referential Integrity...... 112
regular certification exams
    29
Relationship between the
    Developer and DBA
    Certifications............. 32

Reliability and High
   Availability 125
remote Linux machines.. 99
remote location.............. 46
Remote MySQL Servers.. 99
Remote systems............ 113
renamed........................91
replication..................... 42
Replication Capabilities. 112
replication setup............ 42
restarting.......................53
Retaking the Exams........37
Return Result Sets......... 78
revenue margin 109
roadmap 16
rolling feature............... 40
rolling upgrade procedure
   60
root cause.................... 115
row-level locking 67
Row-level Locking 112
Row-level Triggers......... 84
RTOS 117
Run Cluster 43
Running Multiple Nodes .51
running MySQL Cluster . 46
savepoints................ 14, 54
Scalability Characteristics
   114
Scalable Coherent Interface
   56
scalable multi-processor
   systems......................57
Scenarios for Embedding
   MySQL...................... 110
SCI support 46
Self-study...................... 28
separate career tracks 32
separately..................... 62
Server........................... 64
server compilation types.. 17
Server SQL Mode........... 69

server-side stored
   procedures................ 95
shared memory.............. 56
Shared-nothing clustering15
Single Computer.............51
single Table....................77
Single table 92
slave 14
slaves............................ 42
small footprint.............. 68
Spatial data types........... 54
Special Networking........ 43
specialized commands.....47
specific implementation. 66
specific special behavior . 84
specific storage engines.. 68
speed optimizations....... 40
split brain...................... 58
SQL Database Management
   System.......................10
SQL node...................... 45
SQL parser 18
SQL statement...............76
SQL syntax 69
SSL enabled 106
SSL support....................14
SSL Support 106
standalone relational
   database...................126
Start 62
Statement-level Triggers 84
stock installation............27
Stop MySQL Cluster....... 62
storage engine................51
storage engines...............16
Storage Engines........67, 68
Storage Engines Supported
   49
Stored Procedure Accessing
   Tables 76
stored procedures.......... 68
Stored procedures...........13

Stored Procedures Location 75
Stored Procedures' "Raise" Statement 78
Strict mode.....................14
support Cluster.............. 49
supported transactions....67
Synchronization............ 112
synchronous.................. 42
system libraries 11
system shell prompt....... 48
table scans..................... 68
Table Snapshots 91
Table Types change.......105
Tables 95
TCP/IP 43, 46, 56
technical field................ 28
test center locator.......... 30
The Network 18
third-party endorsement .25
Total Cost of Ownership120
Transaction inside a Stored Procedure 83
Trigger............................76
Trigger Calling a Stored Procedure 87
Trigger Updating Tables on Remote Servers 89
triggers 68
Triggers 14
Triggers Accessing a Single/Multiple Tables87
Triggers Calling an External Application............... 89
triggers 'database level' objects 87
Triggers Storage 87
Triggers stored 87

True VARCHAR support .14
tune............................. 116
under development........ 40
Underlying Table is dropped.....................91
undesirable 58
Unicode and Double-Byte character support...... 112
Unique Benefits............. 68
Unix 117
Unix-like operating systems 99
Updatable Views.............14
Updates 63
Updating a View............ 92
Upgrading MySQL 4 Certifications............. 29
User Defined Functions. 112
Uses of MySQL 12
Variable Value 81
Venue 30
Versions of the MySQL Software..................... 49
viable cluster 43
View all Triggers in a Database 86
Viewing All Stored Procedures 75
views 68
web applications.............12
Windows.......................117
WITH RECOMPILE....... 80
work............................. 39
working experience........ 32
XML functions................16
yacc 18
YaSSL library 106

Printed in the United States
70643LV00002B/33